Instantly
A
Widow

Discovery House
PUBLISHERS
BOX 3566 · GRAND RAPIDS, MI 49501

*PUBLISHING BOOKS THAT FEED
THE SOUL WITH THE WORD OF GOD.*

Instantly
A
Widow

by

Ruth M. Sissom

Instantly a Widow
Copyright © 1990 by Ruth M. Sissom

Unless indicated otherwise, Scripture is taken from the
HOLY BIBLE, NEW KING JAMES VERSION.
Copyright © 1983 Thomas Nelson, Inc.
Used by permission of Thomas Nelson, Inc.

Library of Congress Cataloging-in-Publication Data

Sissom, Ruth M.
Instantly a widow/by Ruth Sissom
p. cm.

ISBN 0-929239-33-4

1. Widows—United States—Psychology.
2. Widows—United States—Religious life.
3. Bereavement—Psychological aspects. I. Title
HQ1058.5.U5S57 1990
306.88—dc20   90-3984
                                                              CIP

Discovery House Publishers is affiliated with Radio Bible Class,
Grand Rapids, Michigan

Printed in the United States of America

90 91 92 93 94 / CHG / 10 9 8 7 6 5 4 3 2 1

CONTENTS

FOREWORD

Life changes create stress, and one of the most intensely stressful events is the death of a spouse. Whether the death is an expected one following a long illness or is the result of a sudden illness or accident, no one is ever quite prepared to be the one "left behind." Coping with this new way of life is difficult, to say the least; and as a psychiatrist, I have treated many widows and widowers whose loss triggered depression.

It is important to understand, however, that grief reactions are not clinical depressions; and understanding the stages of grief and recovery will help individuals to work through the process. I have listed these stages below. Although it is not included in this list, I feel it is worth mentioning that "bargaining" is an inherent part of the grief process. This is the point that we reach where we bargain with God by telling Him that if He allows our loved one to live, we will make significant changes in our personal lifestyles.

The remaining stages are as follows:

1. Denial—This is a brief stage where the person cannot believe that it's actually happening.

2. Anger turned outward—The individual is angry toward someone other than himself or herself, perhaps

even toward the person who died. This might even include anger toward God for allowing it to happen.

3. Anger turned inward—This takes place when the person starts feeling somehow responsible for the death and begins blaming himself or herself.

4. Genuine grief—This is the stage when one can actually weep over the loss.

5. Resolution—The person regains his joy for life.

If someone who has lost a spouse becomes non-functional (unable to do daily tasks) for a prolonged period of time or becomes suicidal, that individual should seek the help of a Christian psychiatrist or psychologist. Many survivors find Christian counseling a positive influence, even when the grief has not reached this severity.

Ruth Sissom shares her personal story with us in the following pages. The title, *Instantly a Widow*, is an apt description of the way her life was totally uprooted in just one tragic afternoon.

Ruth vividly describes her thoughts and feelings through each new step she has to take. She shares her most intimate conversations with the Lord so that we can see how He is faithful to provide the strength and the eventual peace that comes through the final stage of resolution. By being so candid, she provides hope and inspiration to each of us.

The message that she imparts to us is that the grief process takes time. We can see through her testimony

God's promise to be near us at all times (Psalm 34:18). We learn that we will never stop loving or remembering our loved one, but we can find a way to go on living a productive and fulfilling life.

Frank Minirth, M.D.

PREFACE

It is winter. During the night fluffy snow fell silently, transforming the barren yard and woods into a winter wonderland. A scarlet cardinal now sits perched near two colorful blue jays on the leafless limb of the wild cherry tree, surveying the contents of the bird feeder.

As I view this peaceful winter scene through my living room window, my mind wanders back to the happy years my husband and I spent here raising our three children. Nine years have passed since his death. Our children are adults now with their own homes, and I am learning to live a meaningful life on my own.

My family has been encouraging me to write of my experiences as a widow, and today I am determined to begin my chronicle.

The whole idea seemed distasteful at first, and I raised many objections. Numerous books had already been written by widows; what would be the benefit of one more? Many people had experienced greater tragedies; perhaps they should write instead of me. Resurrecting the shock, pain, and despair would mean experiencing those emotions again to some degree. Furthermore, I've always been a very private person, and this book would have to be intensely personal, revealing the intimacies of my heart. I continued to rationalize my opposition to the idea.

However, one afternoon, while reading Isaiah 61:3, I became convinced that I should share my story. In that passage God promised this to those who mourned in Zion:

beauty for ashes, the oil of *joy* for mourning, and the garment of *praise* for the spirit of heaviness. God's purpose in bringing beauty, joy, and praise out of mourning was so that He might be glorified as others looked at those upon whom He had showered His blessings. I had heard others talk about "beauty for ashes" many times, but until that afternoon I had never realized the beautiful message in the rest of the verse. Although it was written to Israel, I believe it has an application for Christians today, including me.

I shrink from the valleys in my life. They make me feel fear and foreboding. I don't like ashes, mourning, and heaviness. But after going through some difficult times and looking back on them, I realize they are the way to experiencing the marvelous refreshment from God Himself.

I now have an opportunity to share how God has brought the truth of that verse to pass in my life. I remember the many times I have been inspired to a stronger faith by reading or hearing another's personal experience. Knowing God was with me in my sorrow could give others confidence that God can do for them what He has done for me. Relating how God's strength was "made perfect" in my weakness during bereavement would bring glory to Him.

The purpose for sharing this very personal story has come clearly into focus. I want to glorify the One who is the Source of all comfort, bring hope and encouragement to those who must endure sorrow and loneliness, and give insight to those who sincerely want to comfort the bereaved.

So today I will begin the task of reliving and putting in print the almost inexpressible personal experiences surrounding my widowhood. I choose to tell my story exactly as I recall it happening; to be brutally frank about my emotions and feelings, noble and ignoble.

Certainly every widow's experience is unique and the death of a husband does not necessarily mean overwhelming despair and collapse as it did for me. But since everyone in a lifetime confronts losses of persons and things he or she loves, my story is for everyone. Perhaps some will be inspired and helped by my forthright recollections.

If this book will lead others to praise God, help those who are grieving to gain a fresh perspective, and stimulate courage to pick up the pieces and start over, my efforts will be worthwhile, and I will be grateful.

ONE

Peace in the Midst of Panic

"Mrs. Sissom, STAT!"

"Mrs. Sissom, STAT!"

I rushed to my desk phone and with trembling hands picked up the receiver to answer the urgent call coming over the intercom system of the hospital where I was Director of Education. My mind was racing. What emergency would be on the other end?

"This is Paul. Daddy was repairing Janet's car; it fell on him and he was trapped under it when I came home from school. I raised the car up, got him out, and the ambulance is on the way. He looks terribly blue and Janet and I can't feel his pulse."

"I'll get there as fast as I can," I replied with my heart pounding wildly. "It sounds as if you have the situation under control. Call Carol. I'm on my way."

I was proud and amazed at my seventeen-year-old son's levelheadedness and quick action in the midst of crisis. I wondered how my daughter, Janet, was coping.

I phoned my boss and ran to my car. Speeding from the parking lot, I found my mind racing ahead to what I would find when I reached home.

"*Oh, God,*" I cried in anguish, "*don't let him be paralyzed. He could never cope with having others wait on him. He is strong and independent.*"

He had helped clear virgin wooded land in the hills of Tennessee for farming and was used to lifting heavy stumps, driving stubborn mules, lifting hay racks, milking cows, walking all day behind a plow or cultivator.

"*Oh, God, don't let him be paralyzed, because I can't cope with the burden of caring for a helpless husband. I know that's selfish, but NO, GOD, NO!*"

Suddenly aware of the houses on the side of the road flying by, I glanced at the speedometer; eighty miles an hour! I quickly lifted my foot from the accelerator. *My children could lose both parents in one day. I MUST SLOW DOWN.* Without thinking, back went my foot. *I MUST HURRY.*

"*Oh, God, no. Please make this come out all right,*" I prayed frantically.

The thirteen mile drive home seemed endless as I sped along. About twenty-five minutes after receiving the urgent call from Paul, I reached the long country driveway that wound through the woods. We had purchased this ten acres of land nineteen years before and cleared a spot to build our house.

A rescue vehicle was pulling out. My heart sank. What would I find?

"*Lord, give me strength to face whatever it is.*"

People were standing in the yard. Our dog Fritz was barking anxiously.

"They've taken him to the hospital. Janet rode in the ambulance," Paul informed me.

I called the emergency room. "Is he alive?"

They were evasive. "He is here, we are working on him, come right away."

Paul stayed at the house while my daughter, Carol,

and I drove to the hospital in a silent daze. Janet was in the waiting room crying. I hugged her. We three were told to go into a small room. The young doctor entered. It seemed a face of stone confronted me and a compassionless gaze met the hopeful longing radiating from my eyes.

"We've done all we can do and *he is dead!*"

It seemed he yelled those words that felt like a huge sword cutting me from head to toe. The feeling of a powerful weight crushing down on me took my breath away.

"Do you want to see the body?"

"Yes."

"*No, Mother, don't go!—it's too terrible—don't go!*"

"I need to," I said and walked slowly into the emergency room.

A young male attendant stood in the room. *Why doesn't he leave me alone?*

"Do you want his rings?"

How can he ask me such a thing at a time like this?

"No."

I leaned over and gave Cecil a kiss on his forehead. It was cold, lifeless, unresponsive.

"*OH NO, GOD, NO! HELP ME! I can't believe this is happening.*"

Suddenly it seemed as if the whole world stood absolutely still—no sound—no movement—perfect peace.

"*It's all right My child, I'm with you. Trust Me. Everything will be all right.*"

Time seemed to have stopped. A feeling of peaceful calm assurance I had never before experienced was deep within me. I looked at the clock. It had not stopped even though it felt as if I were in a timeless environment. In the darkest hour of my life, God made His presence known to me in a most marvelous way.

This must be the "peace that passes understanding" God promises to His children. It was completely beyond my comprehension how I could experience absolute perfect peace in the midst of this chaos and emotional upheaval. *I want to stay here forever basking in the warmth of God's peace and love, but my daughters are waiting. I must go. "Thank You, God, for this wonderful assurance that I am Your child and You love me."* It really is true that *"the Lord is near to the brokenhearted and saves those who are crushed in spirit."*

I walked into the hall. Friends were there. One of them hugged me and said, "God never makes mistakes." Those icy cold words plunged like a dagger, tearing into the depths of my heart. I couldn't stand to hear them now.

"Oh, God, I don't believe this is happening. It must be a bad dream. Wake me up. Tell me it's not true."

The nurse came. "You will have to call the funeral home."

Me call! As a nurse, I had always done the calling in cases of death. *What's wrong with her, has she no feelings? How cold and heartless these medical people seem. They are my peers. Did I appear this way to those I cared for at times of death? I certainly hope not!*

My eyes wouldn't focus. I couldn't see the number. The nurse read it for me. *I can't say the words. How can I say, "Come pick up my husband's body?" No, I can't say it. But I have to!*

"God, help me!"

"Please pick up my husband's body at the emergency room," I blurted out.

The clothes were handed to me in a large plastic satchel. They felt like lead as I carried them to the car. We drove home in stunned silence.

Paul came to the door. "He's gone," I said. Tears

welled up in his eyes. Janet began fixing supper. She seemed to have the ability to maintain some measure of order and continuity in our lives even in the midst of panic and despair. The food tasted like cardboard. I struggled to swallow a few bites. I felt numb. I couldn't think clearly or function routinely.

Phone calls began coming. I repeated the unbelievable words, "Yes, he died today."

I called Mother. "We've had a terrible tragedy in our family. Please notify the others."

My sister Marjorie phoned. *How kind she is and willing to share my pain.*

An eerie stillness hovered over us that evening. We said almost nothing to each other. We were stunned, dazed, unable to verbalize our shock and despair.

My wildly pounding heart seemed to vibrate the entire king-size bed. I relived the unbelievable events of the past afternoon over and over the entire night. *How long had he lain there screaming for help with the crushing load on him and no way to escape?* I imagined him struggling, screaming, praying, writhing in pain and agony. If I only could know he didn't suffer a long time. No sleep came. Only pain, disbelief, and shock.

The next morning I met the pastor at the funeral home. "Don't you want to include your children in planning the funeral?" he asked.

"No, I don't want to put them through any more pain than necessary. I'll handle it."

As I sat in the funeral director's office my head was spinning. I kept saying over and over to myself, *I don't believe it, it can't be true. Yesterday at this time he was fine.*

"Wake me up, Lord, this has to be a bad dream. Tell me it's not true."

Just yesterday all was well. This can't *be true. Now that I think about it, yesterday I felt an eerie sensation when Cecil kissed me good-bye as I left for work. I did not realize it was the last kiss he would ever give me.*

"Now select a casket." We walked into a large room with caskets everywhere.

How can I select a casket *for my husband? I can't. But I have to!*

"HELP ME, GOD."

"Are they all so expensive?"

"Don't you have more upstairs?" the pastor asked.

"Yes, this way."

The pastor said that a pine box was good enough for him to be buried in.

My mind is absolutely out of gear, I can't think.

"Help me, Lord, to muster enough mental capacity to make this decision."

As long as I have to do this, I must do it the way I think he would want it.

"This one—the oak."

He loved trees and could name all the kinds. He loved the smell of wood. *I must also consider his family's feelings. They would like a special, beautiful casket.*

My knees were wobbly and my hands were trembling. *A* casket *for my husband, I can't believe it!* When the arrangements were completed I left the funeral home feeling stunned and confused. It seemed as if I were experiencing a horrible dream. I could not make myself believe that I had just arranged the funeral for my husband. He had been alive and well at this time yesterday.

Back at the house I selected the clothes. He would want his Hart, Schaffner & Marx suit. He was so proud he owned one. We had never definitely decided where we would be buried. Now I must make that decision without him and I trembled, hoping I was doing what he would want.

That afternoon I contacted the cemetery owner. I purchased two lots. By buying my lot now I would spare my children this turmoil at my death.

The next morning Jeannette came to the house. I grabbed her and sobbed uncontrollably. "Why," she asked, "would God do such a thing? Why would He take a good husband and father, a faithful church worker?"

"I can honestly say I haven't asked God why," I responded.

I was so glad she allowed me to hang on to her as I shook with sobs and soaked her shoulders with my tears.

Later that day the pastor and his wife met us at the funeral home, just before visiting hours for family and friends.

"I was unable to remove all the bluish coloring from his skin," the funeral director explained.

"Why did he have to say that?" The deep pain pierced me again. *That must mean he suffered a long time.* My insides felt wounded and raw from the constant stabbing pain that was piercing my heart again and again.

Carol, Janet, Paul, and I stood at the casket in continued unbelief and shock. The children were silent.

"He's in heaven," I said.

Friends and family began arriving. "I don't know what to say—this never should have happened—it's not fair—I'm sorry."

Nothing you can say is as comforting as your presence, just being here, your willingness to share our pain. I don't want to hear lots of words—not even words from the Bible. What helps most is your quiet presence, your willingness to listen to how I'm feeling, your hugs, handshakes, your shoulder to cry on if I need it.

Flowers kept arriving. I inspected each one. *How wonderful people are. They do care and desperately want to help.* But how helpless and at a loss they all seemed. They were hurting too, but I could only seem to think of *me* and *my* pain. I was thankful for every act of kindness, but couldn't help thinking of Job's "miserable comforters." *The pain is too deep. No one has enough balm to soothe it.*

"Oh, Lord, help me be a good witness for You. Help me speak to many who come who don't know You."

"He's in heaven," I kept repeating.

I felt a superhuman composure and strength. I was responding as a gracious hostess: greeting, smiling, hugging, thanking people for coming. Inside I felt numb and mechanical. Mentally I was repeating, *this can't be true, I can't believe this has happened.*

In retrospect I am very grateful that God graciously made me so that I was anesthetized and numb in the first stage of my tragic loss. This protected me from having to face the entire reality all at once. It enabled me to get through the first three weeks before the devastating impact of the loss sank in.

At home the eerie silence persisted. Each of us was doing the necessary tasks in a cold, silent, mechanical way. We were stunned with shock and disbelief, walking about in a daze. We hardly spoke to each other. I needed to verbalize my feelings and encourage my children to share theirs, but we seemed unable to put into words the deep pain we felt. We appeared to be trying to protect each other from additional suffering that might be caused by our words. We never did sit down together to talk about how this tragedy was affecting each of us.

Carol was our quiet child and she remained outwardly calm and composed. She slept soundly for ten hours at night and found it hard to keep from napping during the day. The urge to sleep seemed an unconscious attempt to escape facing the tragic reality.

Janet had displayed boundless energy during her growing up years and now she took over the routine tasks of cooking, setting the table, and washing dishes. No doubt her training as a nurse helped her bring some degree of order to this chaotic situation. The day after the funeral she returned to college in Pennsylvania.

Paul always had a curious, inquisitive nature. During this time of crisis he provided stability with his level head and common sense. He had several friends who spent time with him and supported him as he grieved.

Food was delivered, friends called. I was overwhelmed by the kindness and helpfulness. Sympathy cards came by the dozens, money from the neighbors and Cecil's co-workers. *How wonderful these people are.*
"Thank You, Lord."

As we drove into the church parking lot for the funeral, my brother, Phillip, arrived and greeted me with a hug. I responded with a burst of sobs. I couldn't speak. *Thank you for not pushing me away, for just holding me and giving me your kind shoulder to cry on.* Family and co-workers arrived. I tried desperately to control my tears while I greeted guests and thanked them for coming.

The church was so packed for the funeral that extra chairs were put in the back.

"This was not in this man's plans," the pastor said. "Are you who are here ready if your plans should suddenly come to an end?"

I sat in the front row with my children. I wanted to be brave for their sakes but could not hold back the tears that now streamed down my face. I could feel the warm wetness as the tears splashed onto my blouse. *Just three days ago Cecil was in this very place, sitting beside me, singing in the choir, praying, laughing, a picture of health. THIS HAS TO BE A BAD DREAM. How can I ever endure to the end of this service. Words of comfort from the pastor, songs of hope sung by friends and family, soft organ music all seem to make the tears flow faster. I'm a wreck!*

At the end of the service the funeral director came down to the front row to escort me out to the waiting hearse. My face felt hot, swollen, and wet. *I'm glad this service is over! If only I could slip out a side door so I wouldn't have to face these people. I'm so embarrassed that I can't keep from crying.* I looked into the sea of faces as I started back the aisle. All eyes seemed fixed on me. There were tears in many of them. A dark cloud of shock and sadness seemed to encompass the entire congregation. *How deeply do they feel this pain? Can they even begin to realize how "chopped in half" I feel?* An eerie silence prevailed as people left the church. Most of them spoke in hushed tones or not at all.

Mother joined the children and me in the hearse. A kind neighbor came to hug Janet and comfort her. Janet had babysat her children many times. *What a thoughtful, compassionate gesture.* Mother's kind, loving presence helped dispel the icy coldness of the hearse. *We are taking him past his home for the last time. The woods, the barn he built, the memories. It's over for him. My children are being so brave and I'm a wreck. I'm supposed to be the strong one, and I'm falling apart.*

"Help me to be strong, Lord."

The sun peeked through the clouds warming me with a feeling of God's love as we drove into the cemetery. The short graveside ceremony seemed like a blur.

We returned to the church for the dinner lovingly prepared by the ladies. I felt stunned and dazed. *Everyone is laughing, talking, eating, as if nothing is wrong. How can they eat? My stomach feels full of lead. How can I go on?*

I felt enveloped by dark clouds of confusion, in a separate world from those around me.

Unfortunately the anguish that seemed so intense was but a small foretaste of that to come.

TWO

Meanwhile, Where Is God?

I hated to see the nights come. They seemed endless and terrible, filled with nightmares of Cecil's body being crushed while he screamed in agony. I relived the dreadful scene over and over each night for weeks until every ounce of my strength seemed drained from dealing with the terror, guilt, and pain. I would reach across the bed hoping to touch his warm body—*HE'S GONE!* My pounding heart vibrated the bed. *Will I ever be able to sleep again? How can I endure another night?*

I felt like a drowning victim going down the last time. Thoughts of all I must do flooded over me. I kept reiterating my mental list as I lay sleepless: clean out his closet, pay the funeral bill, notify the mortgage company and the bank—so much to do and so little strength.

"Help me, Lord." I want to get all the painful jobs done and behind me. The quicker the better.

During the week following the funeral I stood in front of his closet still stunned in disbelief. Nothing in my experience as a widow was as traumatic as disposing of my husband's personal belongings. *Just five days ago he was wearing these clothes. I must pack them and take them to the*

Salvation Army. Waves of nausea kept sweeping over me. *I CAN'T DO THIS, BUT I HAVE TO. I can't stand to give away the sweaters I knit for him, the top coat and new suit I just bought for him. I'll keep them for now.*

In a special box, I packed his certificate commemorating thirty years of service in state mental health work, three service award pins, his wrist watch, pocket watch, mouth organs, billfolds, New Testament, Bible, shaving mug, pen knives, manicure set, his cuff links, and his silver pen and pencil set. Acute pain pierced me as I handled each item, as the stark reality that he would never use them again shocked my aching heart. Many of these things reflected a life given in service to his fellowman. I put the lid on the box and stored it back in his closet for safe keeping.

I drove to the Salvation Army.

"Will you help me unload?"

"No, just put the things in the outside drop box," I was told. *Doesn't anybody care? I'm exhausted. "Give me strength, Lord."*

I strained, tugged, and lifted with every ounce of strength. Slowly I dragged the last bag out of the car and closed the trunk lid with a thud. I felt weak, shaky, and nauseous, but was glad one painful task was completed.

The next day I decided to withdraw Cecil's money from the credit union to help pay the bills. What I expected to be a simple task turned out to be one of the most physically exhausting and mentally draining experiences of that first week of my widowhood. With confidence I approached the teller and asked to withdraw my husband's money. I was shocked by the teller's reply.

"You can't withdraw credit union funds until the funeral bill is paid and you have power of attorney."

"You must be kidding," I responded. "There's only

two hundred dollars. What if I needed the money to pay the funeral bill?"

"It's the law," she replied. I drove to the county building about twenty miles away. At the county clerk's office I was told that power of attorney was only given when the person is living.

"This is the proper document you need along with another death certificate," the clerk advised.

I walked the two blocks to the courthouse.

"Give me five certificates." *I'm going to make sure I have enough this time. These legal hassles! I feel so ignorant about what to do. Everywhere I go I need a death certificate—back to the court house, another fee, another certificate. Will this ever end?*

There seemed a cruel disrespect associated with all those copies. I could not read the cause of death on that certificate for weeks. I would slowly try to focus my eyes there but each time they would move away swiftly. It was too painful.

I drove the twenty miles to the funeral home to pay the bill, then another twenty miles back to the credit union. I presented the proof that the funeral bill was paid along with the notarized county document giving me authority to withdraw the funds. I was given the money. I climbed into my car and started to drive home.

I'm on the freeway going somewhere but I can't remember where I'm going or why. I must be losing my mind. Where am I? Just keep driving, sooner or later I'll see something familiar. What a terrible empty feeling!—That looks familiar— now I think I know where I am.

"Thank You, Lord . . . *what a stressful day this has been. Without You I don't think I would have made it.*"

It was Easter—only eight days since Cecil had gone to heaven. I opened the car door and stepped onto the church parking lot. I forced one foot ahead of the other. A sweeping nausea flooded over me as I entered the church door where Cecil always stood greeting people and handing out bulletins. I was the only one who had practiced the piano part with the choir for the Easter cantata. There was an atmosphere of joy and great expectation as the congregation anticipated the beautiful music. *I feel absolutely exhausted. I CAN'T HANDLE THIS ASSIGNMENT—BUT I HAVE TO! There is no one else who can play the piano part. The whole church is depending on me—and GOD is depending on me too!*

"Help me, Lord."

Mary came up to the piano and touched me on the shoulder. "This will be a test of God's strength working through you. I'll be praying." Mary had lost a daughter in childbirth not long before. The choir director gave the downbeat. I struck the first chord. A calm settled over me. I was able to concentrate completely on the music in spite of having had extreme difficulty concentrating ever since Cecil's death. All other thoughts cleared from my mind like a curtain rolling back. I felt a clearness of vision and mental acuity. The time flew. It hardly seemed possible that we had completed the entire cantata as I played the concluding notes.

It's over—I did it! "Thank You, Lord."

Two weeks after Cecil's death I went alone to select a gravestone. I was determined to spare my children as much pain as I could. This was only one of a multitude of things requiring my attention under the worst possible emotional circumstances. It seemed so futile to spend money to mark a spot that didn't really contain my husband. He was rejoicing in heaven now. I thought of him worshiping God in unspeakable joy—not lifeless in a cemetery plot. But some things must be done whether they make any logical sense or not, I decided. So rebelling with every fiber of my being, I selected a simple, small marker.

With the selection of the grave marker behind me, I knew that somehow life had to go on and I had to force myself back into the routine. So after three weeks away, I returned to my job at the hospital. I shut my office door and looked at the phone that had brought the tragic news. *I don't want to see anyone—please leave me alone.* But people wanted to help.

"You could get married again, but it's not the same." Goodhearted Laura, a widow herself, tried to comfort me with those words and a hug. People kept coming, trying to comfort. *I can't take this. I'm crying. I can't let people see me cry.*

"You must eat," my co-worker advised as we approached the cafeteria line.

Can't she understand the knot in my stomach? I have this strange notion that I MUST NOT EAT. I must lose weight so people will see some outward manifestation of how much I'm hurting inside. That's what I'll do. I realize it's self-pity, but somehow I have to let people know how badly I'm hurting. I can keep smiling and saying, "I'm doing fine," but as I lose weight they will begin to feel sorry for me. I knew I was falling into the trap of self-pity, but I seemed unable to help myself out of it.

Friends drove in the driveway the evening after my second day of work.

"Will you come in?"

"No," they responded. "We will just visit a couple of minutes."

My body began to shake. My knees wobbled. *Are they never going to leave? Don't they understand how physically exhausted I am?*

Returning to the house after they left, my body began shaking violently as if with chills. The next morning I stood at the side of the bed with my whole body trembling. My legs felt like rubber. I stumbled to the phone, bumping into walls and furniture.

"I'm ill and on my way to the doctor," I informed my boss.

The doctor examined me.

"You cannot work like this. You need the summer off," he advised. "These symptoms are from the severe stress your body is dealing with."

What a relief to know I don't have to cope with my job right now.

"Thank You, Lord."

I returned home and read through the sympathy cards and letters again. I found them comforting. I could read them when I was emotionally ready. They didn't demand the instant response of a phone call or face to face encounter.

I found myself sinking deeper each day into the shadows of despair. I had come to the lowest point in my sorrow. It was four weeks after Cecil's death. Physically ill, emotionally drained, and mentally exhausted, I was sitting in the recliner that we had given Cecil for Christmas.

"God, where are You?" I cried out. *"I can't find You. My prayers are falling on deaf ears. You have left me all alone. You are gone. I can't take any more. I feel like I'm in a deep well and can't climb out. There's no use going on living."*

I don't want to go out of the house; someone might see me. I don't want to see anyone and have to talk. June is offended because she invited me to breakfast and I didn't go. Can't anyone understand what an effort it is just to open my eyes and face another day—to make myself get out of bed and get dressed? I CAN'T HANDLE ANY MORE THAN THAT RIGHT NOW. I was doing better two weeks ago.

How do people think you can get over a tragic death so quickly? They just don't understand. I'd like to tell them, "Don't give advice—like 'you need to think about moving from that secluded place in the country, return to work at once, take a trip, go back to college, find an apartment'—or try to force me to do anything. Just be there when I need you. Just listen and let me ramble on, even if it doesn't make sense.

"Let me tell you how guilty I feel because I was not at home when the accident happened; for asking God not to leave Cecil paralyzed because I was selfish and didn't want the burden of caring for a handicapped husband. Let me share my guilt of past words and deeds that I can never retract and make amends for; the guilt of rushing through life instead of treasuring more moments together, relaxing, taking a trip or sharing a night out. Let me explain how I was the one who never wanted to 'waste' money on pleasure, always looking forward to 'someday' when we would be able to afford all the pleasures we missed while raising our children. Let me tell you how sad I feel when I think about Cecil's retirement that was coming in just fifteen months. How he was going to take me on a much-anticipated vacation out West and we were going to begin to enjoy life together. Now that is gone forever. It is a stark reality that all our plans and dreams are gone forever. He is not coming back—EVER!

"There is no one in the world now who loves me more than he loves anyone else, and chances are there never will be—no one to whom I am first. The companionship, love, and commitment are gone. The bed we shared so long is empty—a constant, gaping reminder that I am totally alone. Yes, let me tell you how I feel and don't offer me a handful of easy answers. There are none."

"Oh, God," I cried, "I've failed You. The thing I wanted most through all this was not to fail You. I wanted to be so strong—to rise above the pain, fear, panic, and confusion and

show others I have a faith that doesn't crumble no matter what happens. I wanted to smile and sing with confidence It Is Well With My Soul, *but instead I'm afraid, weak, and utterly distraught. I feel You have forsaken me. I feel like a terrible failure. 'The joy of the Lord is your strength' is meaningless to me now. I'm trying so hard to put on a good front and not let people know how I'm hurting inside. Then some word or song or picture triggers the grief and the sorrow flows over me like an ocean wave, and I'm lost in despair. Where are You, God? I've come to the bottom. If You give me one more thing, however tiny, I CAN'T TAKE IT!"*

I had the false notion, explained by Granger Westburg in *Good Grief*, "that a person with strong faith does not grieve and is above this sort of thing . . . . The Scriptures, both Old and New Testaments, see grief as normal and potentially creative . . . . Through the centuries people who have been able to face grief in the knowledge that God still cares about them have said that grief can be counted among the great deepening experiences of life."

I, too, would ultimately agree that this grief, which seemed absolutely overwhelming now, was the means of drawing me into a closer relationship with God than I had ever known before. For it is when we realize our helplessness without God that He can draw us closer. I was driven to more intense Bible study and prayer and a much greater dependence on God as my protector and provider now that my earthly husband was gone.

I sat silently in the recliner for some time in deep despair. Then I felt an urge to get my Bible. *I'll read in Job.* As I read Job 1:1, I was impressed by the fact that Job was faithful to God and yet he suffered unbelievable loss. *The fact that he was a believer did not lessen his pain and it won't lessen mine either. I can't gloss over my heartache in the guise of* belonging to God. I can't smile and say Cecil is in heaven and all his troubles are over and then go about singing God's praises. Being overwhelmed with grief is a very human reaction. God understood Job's despair. Can He understand mine?

Imagine this! I feel just like Job did in chapter 23 verses 8 and 9:

Look, I go forward, but He is not there,
And backward, but I cannot perceive Him;
When He works on the left hand, I cannot behold Him;
When He turns to the right hand, I cannot see Him.

"You and I feel the same, Job." I can't find God. Where is He? I feel absolutely forsaken. I'll read on—verse 10:

But He knows the way that I take;
When He has tested me, I shall come forth as gold.

Suddenly a calm assurance enveloped me—an awareness of His presence. "THANK YOU, GOD! You do understand. You are with me. Someday this will all make sense. Give me strength to carry on."

Little by little He began to give me an answer to that prayer.

THREE

Healing Memories

From the moment I heard the news of my husband's tragic death, I experienced a dreadful, unsettled feeling that the whole world was crumbling under my feet. I became consumed with an overpowering desire to find something of my past roots that was still solid, strong, lasting.

I remembered how God had told His people through Jeremiah that they would find rest for their souls if they would walk in the good ways of their old paths.

I had an intense longing to visit my childhood home. I needed to know that it had not disappeared and left me.

My good friend from nursing school days invited me to spend a day with her. This gave me a perfect excuse to travel in the direction of the farm where I had grown up. I decided not to tell anyone—just take a short side trip on the way.

It was a beautiful day in May as I headed north toward Bad Axe, Michigan. Just beyond Marlette I turned east on the gravel road leading to the farmhouse. On the right I noticed Mrs. Wellwood's house was still there, the porch sagging and unpainted. When I was seventeen I had scurried up on that porch, soaking wet after a cloudburst drenched me as I rode my bike home from my job at the bakery. Mrs. Wellwood had invited me in and given me a dry dress to wear home.

How I hoped the family farmhouse would still be there! My heart raced with anticipation as I crested Boyne hill and saw it in the distance. The place where I was born and raised—the house that had protected us from blinding blizzards and fierce electrical storms, where we laughed, cried, loved, and prayed—the barn where I helped milk cows—the fields where I helped plant and harvest crops—it was still here! This was the precious spot where I had felt totally loved, cared for, and secure.

Suddenly I was encompassed with the sensation of stability my heart had been longing for. Surrounded by a pleasant nostalgia, I slowly approached what had once been home. The years rolled away and I was a little girl again.

The white wood siding and black trimmed windows were the same. Looking at the dining room window over the front porch, I remembered Mother rocking all of us by that window in the chair with the broken rocker while she sang *Trust and Obey*. Inside that window was the room where Mother read the Bible and we prayed. I could not remember missing even one day of family worship in all my growing up years.

I remembered the time we had six baby ducks in a cardboard box behind the range. One morning in the middle of the prayer they began quacking loudly. Phillip and I snickered and were severely reprimanded by Daddy for our irreverence.

Another morning, rain was pouring down the sides of the roof onto the porch as we knelt to pray. Mother began as was her custom, "Thank you, Lord, for this beautiful day."

"Beautiful?" interrupted Daddy, unable to restrain

Instantly A Widow

himself. To a farmer depending on sunny weather to complete the harvesting of his crops it was anything but beautiful. Phillip and I smiled at each other. We realized that Mother's thinking was that every day was a gift from God. "This is the day that the Lord has made. We will rejoice and be glad in it," was her motto.

In that same room stood the range that warmed us and baked Mother's crusty brown loaves of whole wheat bread. I could almost smell the glorious aroma and taste the steaming crusts spread with homemade butter and brown sugar that Mother gave us for a treat. I remembered how the range stood boxed in wood crates for weeks and how we all begged Daddy to put it into operation. Finally the day came. The fire was built and as the first waves of warmth cheered us, we all joined hands and danced around the new stove.

My eyes moved to the window of the living room. The piano had stood there. For a good time we sat around the piano and sang while Daddy played his mouth organ and one of us played the piano. We would pop a big dishpan full of homegrown popcorn to climax our evening together. I recalled that one dark night, as sharp cracks of lightning and deep rolls of thunder filled the sky, Mother had sat on the piano bench praying for our safety with us children gathered around her.

The kitchen window reminded me of the small pot-bellied wood stove that stood just inside the doorway. We slept in brass beds piled high with handmade quilts in the unheated upstairs of the frame farmhouse. On cold winter mornings it took courage to throw back the covers and face a new day. But we would dash down the creaky wood stairs to the red hot, pot-bellied little stove waiting to warm us. Each of us wore a fire brand on our back—the price paid for overindulging in the comforting warmth.

My eyes moved next to the upstairs windows, to the bedroom that Marjorie and I shared. I would get to bed first, wrap up in all the warm covers and fight with Marge for them when she came to bed. They had to be made of strong material or they would have torn right down the middle from our constant tugs of war. I liked to cuddle. Marge did not. One night in desperation she unscrewed the handle from the dust mop, laid it in the middle of the bed and dared me to cross over it. I didn't dare!

In that same room one night long ago, I had awakened to Phillip's bloodcurdling yell, "Help, help, there's a man in my room." Mother marched bravely up the creaky stairs to find that it had all been a bad dream. Paralyzed with fear, I had lain stiff as a poker the rest of the night, unable to move a muscle.

Surveying the front yard I noticed the maple tree that had finally grown tall after Molly, our faithful farm horse, was no longer there to straddle the tree and lurch forward and backward while the tree top scratched her stomach. The snowball bush was still spread over the front fence. I remembered how Mother gave us permission to pick the dying blooms and have a snowball fight on the Fourth of July each year. What fun we had! Just over the west fence stood the old apple tree looking gnarled and twisted from the onslaughts of severe weather it had withstood for many years.

The long red machine shed looked the same. I wondered if the words Daddy had written were still on the interior wood wall: "Ruth hand pumped all the water for the cement used in building this shed."

The tall hip-roofed barn had been repainted deep red. I recalled the night Marjorie and Phillip climbed to the very peak and then sent me to bring Mother from the house to see their daring feat. Trembling with fear, Mother ordered them to come down immediately. Unable to watch, she retreated to the house and promptly went to her knees in prayer until they were safely down.

I could see the gravel pit hill in the distance. I recalled how Phillip had cut his forehead on the barbed-wire fence as he flew down that hill in our homemade wood sled with the crooked runner. That hill was also the scene of much fun on Sunday afternoons as we pushed the family buggy to the top, jumped in and enjoyed a jouncing ride to the bottom.

One of our favorite pastimes was walking on a large steel barrel, rolling it as we went. John had the unhappy experience of slipping on the shiny steel, falling and knocking out his three front teeth. We were all thankful for the modern invention of the partial plate and soon John looked almost as good as new again. But, one night, while Mother was helping him overcome a bout of the flu, she realized, with consternation, that she had flushed the expensive new plate into the septic tank. New partials could be made for a price, which produced a family financial crisis, but before long John's smile was restored.

I thought about the old car we used to drive. Mother started praying for a better car so we could be sure to attend church regularly. To our surprise, Uncle Alfred drove up in his shiny black Chevrolet one sunny afternoon from his home fifty miles away. He had brought the Chevy to us and was going to take our old car to trade in on a new one. We were overjoyed. Mother's prayer had been answered.

I lingered in the warmth of those happy memories. My childhood life on the farm seemed, in retrospect, a simpler, kinder time in a plain, old-fashioned place. A feeling of stability enveloped me. Deep roots were here, inescapable and restorative. I had rediscovered those precious memories of home and family, respect and dignity, diligence, order, love, loyalty, and trust in God.

As I headed back toward the highway I could visualize myself in past years riding my bike down this very road to work in the bakery, to do housework and mow lawns for the neighbors in order to earn tuition money for nursing school. How thankful I felt for the values my parents had instilled within me: the dignity of work and the necessity of determination in striving for a worthy goal.

Turning north on the highway I thought about my life since leaving the farm. Following my graduation from nursing school, Cecil and I had married and within three years we had two beautiful daughters. Times were hard. I worked part time at the hospital and Cecil picked up evening and night jobs to supplement our income. After Janet was born he fished in a nearby lake to put free protein on the table while I became as creative as possible with a twenty-five pound bag of flour.

When Paul was born we decided the place to raise our family was in the country. We bought ten acres of wooded land. The girls and I helped clear a spot for our house among the trees. We stood in the snow and roasted hot dogs in the fire from the brush piles while we laughed and dreamed of our new home.

We wanted our children to experience events from our childhood days so we involved them in gardening, canning food for the winter, churning butter in Mother's old-fashioned crock churn with the wooden dasher, hatching baby chicks (using a setting hen), and helping to care for our laying hens that provided us with tasty brown eggs. We bought a Shetland pony with cart and harness. Olive never seemed to tire of taking us for rides on the country roads. Money had been scarce and life had been hard at times, but

Instantly A Widow

we managed to build many happy memories as a family along the way. These memories were as fresh in my mind as if they had happened yesterday.

My mind raced from the memories of the past to the present. Carol had recently completed three years of college and had a good job. Janet was a licensed practical nurse and attending Bible college. Paul was soon to graduate from high school. I thought about the joy our children had added to our marriage. Next to our relationship with Christ, our children were our greatest joy. Cecil was particularly proud of them. He often pointed out the organist to visitors who attended our church and explained that she was his daughter, Carol. He told them that Janet and Paul taught Sunday school, that they both played the piano and sang in the choir. In fact, I thought he bragged about our children too much, and I often reminded him that all the good in any of us is because of the grace of God.

As I continued driving through the north country, I felt a reviving of my spirit from the vast treasure house of memories that I had unlocked. The cruel sting of death could remove my husband from me physically, but the memories of the life we had shared would live on. I sensed new steadiness, strength, and determination. Somehow, hidden within those pleasant memories was an immortality I could understand.

The stability I gained from this day would help me meet the challenges yet to come.

FOUR

Beginning the Long, Uphill Climb

It was Anne Morrow Lindberg who said, "It isn't for the moment that you are struck that you need courage, but for the long uphill climb." I became acutely aware of this truth as every step of progress I made in adjusting to my husband's death seemed to be followed by at least two steps backward.

As the dreary weeks dragged on, life continued to seem badly shattered, and things I once had enjoyed were now drab and pointless. A pinch of confidence gained today was predictably followed by a wave of gloom for several tomorrows. Just when I thought my emotional ups and downs were leveling off, I would burst into tears. These teary outbursts came about as a result of hearing a song about sorrow, a sermon about heaven, or seeing a person or thing that reminded me of a happy experience shared with my husband. The emotional turmoil was devastating.

"Take the Twenty-Third Psalm," Aunt Eleanor had written, "and everywhere there is a personal pronoun insert your own name." With faltering speech I tried it. "The Lord is Ruth's shepherd. Ruth shall not want. He makes Ruth to lie down in green pastures. He leads Ruth beside the still waters.

He restores Ruth's soul. He leads Ruth in the paths of righteousness for His name's sake. Yea, though Ruth walks through the valley of the shadow of death, Ruth will fear no evil; for You are with Ruth; Your rod and Your staff, they comfort Ruth. You prepare a table before Ruth in the presence of Ruth's enemies. You anoint Ruth's head with oil; Ruth's cup runs over. Surely goodness and mercy shall follow Ruth all the days of her life; and Ruth will dwell in the house of the Lord forever." Over and over I repeated this and it brought comfort.

Still periods of doubt, fear, and sorrow engulfed me. I could really relate to the line in the hymn *It Is Well With My Soul* that says "sorrows like sea billows roll." Many times a word, a song, an event, or seeing a husband hugging his wife would trigger that grief, and the sea billows would come rolling over me, drowning me with sadness.

Holidays and special family events also triggered the wave-like experiences of tearful longing. Our twenty-seventh anniversary came four weeks after Cecil's death. Paul's high school graduation and open house, a month later, caused me to wonder why God didn't allow Cecil to live to share in this important milestone of our son. He would have been so proud. A week later was Father's Day and one month later Cecil's birthday.

"Help me, Lord," I prayed often as I struggled to keep back the ever-present tears.

"I hope the Lord allows me to live to finish building my barn." *Strange that Cecil would have said those words just a short time before his death.* It was almost as if he had a foreboding that he might not live to complete it. Sadness smothered me as I watched our carpenter friend, Jack, install the tracks and hang the doors. *If only he could have lived to see his difficult project completed.*

I had never shared Cecil's enthusiasm for junk collecting and I couldn't wait to restore some order and neatness to the barnyard. Paul and I lifted, pulled, tugged, bagged, and put things in the barn. Then we hired a wrecker to remove the worn out green Oldsmobile and blue pick-up truck. Paul raked and planted grass. As I was cleaning the yard behind the barn, I felt a hand on my shoulder and a presence.

"What are you doing with all my treasures?"

I turned slowly. *Is Cecil here?—No one is here. What an eerie feeling. I must be losing my mind.*

I kept dreaming at night. Cecil was sitting on the edge of the bed getting dressed. He seemed so real—*Of course he's real! Why do you think anything is wrong? He's here, everything is all right.* I woke suddenly. *He is not here. HE IS GONE!*

I looked out toward the barn. My heart skipped a beat. *There's Cecil in the shadows—see—he's moving—I'll call him—maybe he will come.* I called. He didn't come. *HE IS GONE!*

It was the middle of the night; I heard my name called loud and clear—it was Cecil's voice. "Here I am." *I heard him, I HEARD HIM—HE'S HERE!* I called again. He didn't answer. *No, he's not here. HE IS GONE!* The violent struggle between disbelief and painful reality raged on. Intellectually I knew Cecil was never coming back, but emotionally I was totally unable to accept it.

My thinking. I can't think straight. Nothing is making sense. I've always been a logical person. "Oh no, God, don't let me lose my mind." *What is happening? I'm going crazy, my mind is snapping—all this financial and legal business—all those decisions—the dreams—I can't cope.*

"Yes, you can," assured Gloria, my nurse friend. "For twenty-seven years every thought and decision considered another person, and now that person is gone. Your entire thought pattern has to change. Tell yourself, 'I'm rearranging my thinking. I will give myself time. It's a slow process. Relax, I am *not* going crazy.' "

"Thank you, Gloria." That advice gave me something to hang on to. It helped to stabilize me when my thoughts made no sense.

My mental confusion was part of the gradual adaptation to the sudden and final separation from my loved one. The ultimate, total separation was too overwhelming to comprehend or accept all at once. By holding on to images, memories, and experiences of Cecil's presence, I was *gradually* saying good-bye.

I was dealing with this sad parting, bit by bit, in a process much like leaving a loved one for a long journey. The traveler embraces and stands looking and longing, then embraces again until the final parting. He walks away, looks back, embracing from a distance with eyes and words of farewell. Then, at the door of the train or plane, he pauses again and turns to wave yet another good-bye. And then, as the train or plane begins to move, he looks and waves from the window until, out of sight, he is left only with memories. But in idle moments, and especially at night, the traveler is reunited with his loved one in his imagination. And so it is with the harsher and more final parting through death. I could only stand the pain of parting through these gradual good-byes.

I began to realize that there are hundreds of daily activities that link one with a spouse: preparing meals, getting off to work, holidays, recreational activities, financial matters. And all these are seriously disrupted and disorganized when the spouse dies. Yet these are part of the fabric of daily life, the simple things one does with, for, or because of the other person. As in a war-torn area, I found that many of the familiar and taken-for-granted signposts and starting points of my daily life were no longer there. Eating meals together, sharing a hug and kiss, riding to work together, sitting together in church, these were a few of the activities that I missed. Life seemed empty now as I trudged on alone. I needed months to grasp the full scope of this disruption. I would start to set my husband's place at the table, or select his favorite cereal when shopping, or hurry into the house to tell him the vegetables we had planted in the garden were popping through the ground. Suddenly I would face the startling realization that he was gone and never coming back.

But our culture seems to deprive the mourner of the time and support needed to reorganize behavior and activities during this period of grief. We seem to be expected to resume our ordinary activities, show no public evidence of our grief, and carry the burden of our loss stoically and alone. Years ago, people grieved more openly. Men wore black armbands and widows wore black veils for six months to a year so that everyone was reminded daily of their loss.

While I was still dealing with my grief, I had the opportunity to hear a Jewish Rabbi present Judaism's observance of mourning practices. Acknowledging the intensity of the first week of grief, bereaving Jews are directed to remain at home, to weep and lament. Pre-funeral visits from friends are discouraged because the mourner is inconsolable at this time and must devote himself exclusively to his acute grief. The Talmud instructs, "One should not comfort the mourner while his dead lies before him." Friends are encouraged to visit immediately after the burial and through the remainder of the first week but to talk with the bereaved only of his loss. They bring food, relieving the bereaved of daily household tasks and freeing him to grieve. For the remainder of the first month, the mourner resumes only the most essential tasks of ordinary life.

Throughout the first year, he is expected to grieve and express his grief publicly in a prescribed fashion as he is progressively, but gently, urged to resume his ordinary activities. By the end of the year, he is expected to resume his life in full but to observe each anniversary of the death. I was impressed by the patient understanding way in which Judaism dealt with their bereaved. Christians could learn much from these practices.

I had been granted a leave of absence from work for the summer and my home was in a peaceful environment conducive to meditation and reminiscing. I thought about a nurse acquaintance who had lost her husband in a car accident. She was left with two small boys to raise. How would she cope with such a heavy load? How was my neighbor doing who had never written a check or paid the bills before his wife's death? I knew a minister's wife who had recently lost her husband. She had a teenage son. She had always lived in a parsonage and had never been employed. Now she was battling almost impossible odds as she sought a job in mid-life with no work experience. She was faced with finding and paying for a place to live for herself and her son. I had to be thankful that my situation was not nearly as critical as these other grieving persons I knew.

"Use your time off this summer to work through your grief," the doctor advised. "Many people immediately return to work and make a conscious effort to shut out the unpleasant thoughts. Grief is work, hard work, but the loss must be wrestled with and all the emotions surrounding it must be faced honestly. Find someone with whom you can share your deepest feelings, who will be understanding and nonjudgmental." My daughter, Carol, listened patiently to my expressions of sadness and longing. She was my best listener.

God was my best comforter. Time after time I opened my Bible to find just the words I needed to soothe my aching heart. I was amazed at the amount of Scripture that is devoted to consoling God's children. Suddenly these verses were leaping off the pages at me and taking on a fresh and very personal meaning. In addition to Psalm 23, a few of the passages that became especially precious to me were:

"He heals the brokenhearted, and binds up their wounds" (Psalm 147:3).

"When you pass through the waters, I will be with you; and through the rivers, they shall not overflow you: when you walk through the fire, you shall not be burned; nor shall the flame scorch you. For I am the Lord your God the Holy One of Israel, your Savior . . ." (Isaiah 43:2–3).

"But He knows the way that I take: when He has tested me, I shall come forth as gold" (Job 23:10).

As I turned to *Our Daily Bread* devotional readings I was astonished at the relevance of the meditations to my situation. These messages had been written months before by someone who didn't even know I existed, and yet God used that person to write messages of hope and comfort just at the right time to calm my troubled heart.

One minute I would be basking in the warmth of God's comfort, and the next thing I knew I was plunged into deep despair. I hated this emotional roller coaster I was riding, but I was powerless to stop it.

Sitting in a Sunday evening church service, I suddenly became conscious of my rapidly pounding, erratic heartbeat. I felt weak and dizzy. I managed to make my way to another room. With my head lying limply on my arms, I asked, *"Oh, God, will I ever feel strong, well, and happy again?"* "In everything give thanks," came to my mind. The pastor's wife had seen me leave and came to sit with me. "I can't possibly understand the reason for Cecil's death or how I can be thankful, but I've thanked God because His Word says to," I told her.

Little by little I began to realize how I could give thanks *in* this situation—not *for* it, at least not yet. I could give thanks because God was with me in the trial and had promised never to forsake me (Hebrews 13:5), and because He had provided me with a home, wonderful children, a job, a supportive church family, and, most of all, His comforting Word and presence. When the depression and despondency flowed over me, I attempted to counteract it by recalling my "Thanksgiving List."

Looking about me, it seemed that other widows were courageously starting over as if nothing had happened, while I trudged along at a snail's pace in my quest to adjust, accept, and chart a new course. Even a trip to the grocery store evoked waves of tearful longings for the companionship of my husband who loved to help select items and always carried the grocery bags for me.

I had grown up in the era when the highest calling for a woman was to be wife, mother, and homemaker. This was always my first priority. When all this was suddenly gone I felt afraid, abandoned, useless.

I remember vividly the moment the painful reality came crashing down on me that my role in life had been completely uprooted. I was riding in the back seat of the car with Mother. I looked at her and thought: she's a widow and so am I.

I'M A WIDOW! I CAN'T BELIEVE IT! How am I to act? Am I supposed to wear my rings or put them in a drawer?

Will married women see me as a threat? I began noticing that the world is organized for couples—tables at restaurants surrounded by chairs in multiples of twos, travel rates for couples, church social events such as canoe trips for couples and sweetheart banquets. Funny I'd never noticed this before. I felt like a tag along, a fifth wheel, an extra who never really fit anywhere. *I've lost my identity as a person. I'm only a statistic. A widow statistic!*

FIVE

Accepting—Adjusting

Questions kept filling my mind about what Cecil was experiencing, even though my friends were telling me he was ecstatically happy and at peace. I knew that to be absent from the body is to be present with the Lord (2 Corinthians 5:8), but I also knew God wipes tears from the eyes in heaven (Revelation 7:17; 21:4).

Those who have died must have tears when God comes to wipe them away. That indicates that God deals with them as a tender father who finds his child in tears, comforts him, and wipes his tears away. Is Cecil sharing my anguish of loss and guilt? Why should this wrenching separation that is so painful to me be painless to my husband? I've always believed that the Christian would instantly pass into perfection and peace at the moment of death, but now I'm not sure. It must be that bereavement results in tears that are, after a time, forever wiped away by God.

An intense struggle continued to rage within me. I desperately wanted to rise above the despair and display a victorious Christian spirit. Outwardly I could maintain composure most of the time and fool acquaintances, but periods of overwhelming grief were evident to those closer to me. I *could not* put the pain of Cecil's death behind me and go forward victoriously with God no matter how hard I tried! I felt like a miserable failure to my loving Heavenly Father. The pain of that failure kept plaguing me constantly until it seemed as bad as the sorrow over my husband's death.

It was during a Bible study class that I began to sense some relief from this anguish. Someone quoted, " 'My grace is sufficient for you, for *My strength is made perfect in weakness.*' Therefore most gladly I will rather boast in my infirmities, that the power of Christ may rest upon me . . . . For when I am weak, then I am strong." I began to understand that it is in the "impossible" situations, when we are weak, that God is best able to display Himself through us. My devastating grief was an opportunity for Christ to manifest His sufficiency through me. This realization was a turning point for me.

"I give my weakness and failure to You, Lord. Use me to demonstrate Your strength, power, and grace."

It was painfully humbling to admit the frailty of my own self and my need for utter dependence on God. I must let God take my anguish and use it in some unexplainable way to accomplish something beautiful for Himself.

It gave me tremendous pain to be near the place in the yard where Cecil had died. I might see some of his blood. The tragic scene kept filling my mind. As I thought of him lying there, clouds of doubt about his salvation encompassed me. *Why is this uncertainty overwhelming me?* Try as I might to chase those fearful thoughts from my mind, I couldn't squelch them. The mental torment raged on. Just when I thought I could stand it no longer, my kind Heavenly Father brought peace through the following incident my friend Jane shared with me.

"I remember the last time I talked to Cecil," Jane told me. "I was putting on my coat at church and he came over and said, 'Don't give up on your husband. Keep praying. My wife didn't give up on me. She prayed seven years for me before I finally accepted the Lord.' "

"Thank You, Lord, for this testimony from his own lips that he belonged to You."

Two months after Cecil's death the marker was placed on his grave and I was asked to go see it and confirm my satisfaction with it. As I entered the cemetery I noticed other grave markers. Some folks had lived long lives and others had been very young when death claimed them. There was a freshly dug grave with a canopy over it. Momentarily I felt acute pain thinking about the anguish someone would experience that day as they laid a loved one to rest. I could scarcely look at the cold marble slab. At that moment, in spite of seeing his name there, this all seemed impossible and unreal. I stooped to pull longer grass away from the marker and used my garden tools to plant some bright cheery flowers. They reminded me of life and hope. I envisioned Cecil in heaven, happy and safe.

During that first summer, friends confronted me with much well-meaning advice:

"You're too young to spend your remaining years in loneliness. You must think about remarriage."

"You should find another woman to live with you."

"It's not safe in the country alone."

"Move into an apartment."

"All that yardwork is too much."

I had read that it was not wise to make any major decisions for at least a year after the death of a spouse. I was determined to follow that advice, so I ignored all the suggestions from my friends.

ACCEPTING—ADJUSTING   *43*

"We are having a church party at our house, please come and join us," Jane invited. "It will be informal and fun."

"You need to get out and participate in some social activities," my friends urged. "Be sure to come."

Reluctantly I agreed to go. We played word games and guessing games. My stomach tightened into a knot when the next game was announced. My palms became sweaty. I considered running up the stairs and out the door to my car, but I didn't know where Jane had put my coat. In this game, one husband and wife sat in the middle of the floor while the other guests sat around them in a circle. The couple was to consult together and then agree on the answers to questions asked by the host.

What am I supposed to do? I'm the only one without a husband. I want to escape, but there's no way to do it gracefully. If I don't join in there won't be enough to play the game, and they are all excited about it.

"Help me make it through this evening, Lord."

My turn is next, what will I do? I feel absolutely sick to my stomach.

"You can borrow my husband for your turn," Jane assured me.

I hardly knew her husband. The other couples had hugged, held hands, and played affectionately during their turns. How embarrassing for me and Jane's husband.

"Your turn, Ruth."

I hesitated and then took my place. To this day I don't remember anything from that point until the game was over. Finally the party ended and I was driving home alone. Tears were streaming down my face.

I will NEVER, NEVER go to another party where there are couples. I know Jane thought she was being kind to offer me her husband, but that was devastating. I'll just become a social cripple, it's better than going through this.

"I'll pick you up and we will go shopping. It will make you feel better to buy some new clothes."

I didn't want to go shopping, but I went anyway as I had no heart to counter Carol's kind offer. I knew she was trying to bolster my spirits and sincerely longed to see me happy again. So off we went to the Tall Shop and selected a summer suit. It fit fine, but as I approached the triple mirror, the shock from the image I saw made me involuntarily step backward. The suit was bright and colorful, appropriate for a high-spirited woman with a merry heart.

I can't wear this, it gives a false impression. Can't anyone understand how my heart is still aching? I want people to realize how deep the wound is, to grieve with me. NO! I CAN'T WEAR IT! Black would blend perfectly with my mood.

"You look lovely. That's the perfect color for you. What a perfect fit!" The saleslady heaped flattering compliments on me.

In total opposition to my heart-cry I succumbed and left with my new suit. It hung in the closet most of that summer.

I had always been self-sufficient. While Cecil worked two jobs I tried to handle all the emergencies at home. But he was always there when things got beyond me. He could repair the car, water pump, or lawn mower. He bargained with car dealers about the terms of the sale. Repair men and builders dealt more with him than with me. Now I was confronted with the purchasing, maintaining and repairing of the car, lawn mower, roto tiller, water pump, and sump pump in addition to the appliances, equipment, plumbing, and furnishings of our home. Salesmen, repair men, and financial advisors seemed to view me as naive, a pushover. Many of them seemed to feel that I wasn't intelligent enough to understand, so why waste time with me? I wanted explanations, answers, and lots of facts before making decisions for purchases and repairs. I felt overwhelmed with the multitude of decisions to be made. I asked questions of Paul and men from church. I began praying, "You are my husband now, Lord, give me wisdom." It helped to deal with one thing at a time—only what was necessary today instead of worrying about all that needed attention in the next year. The world seemed cruel and cold without the protective buffering of my husband.

In sharp contrast to the heartless, God provided concerned church men who painted my house and a kind neighbor who was always available to repair the water pump, replace the sump pump, or shovel me out of a snowbank.

I purchased a new roto tiller. It was delivered unassembled with pages of instructions.

"Help me, Lord," I prayed, *"to put this together."*

I struggled with each laborious step from connecting wheels and handles all the way to filling and wiring the battery. Imagine my surprise and glee when it started with the first turn of the key!

"If I can do that," I thought, *"I can tackle most anything."*

"You look nice today," Sandy commented.

She would never realize what a tremendous lift that gave me. I felt I could never look nice again. I had aged terribly in just a few short weeks.

"How do people who are not Christians handle tragic death?" I asked my pastor.

"Many fall completely apart and have emotional breakdowns. Some visit the grave continually for months or years to weep and mourn. Some keep obsessively occupied while denying the reality of the death and attempt to crowd out the possibility of wrestling with the grief."

Before Cecil died I had no idea losing a husband caused such devastating despair. I admired the courageous widows I knew and felt a new closeness to them. I felt convinced I would have had an emotional breakdown apart from God's sustaining presence, love, and care. Gradually I was sensing "a peace that cometh after sorrow, of hope surrendered, not of hope fulfilled. A peace that looketh not upon tomorrow, but calmly on a tempest that is stilled."

"This is a good time to set some goals," my pastor advised.

For me this was a painful process, as it focused me on the future which seemed full of suspense and insecurity.

I'll start with just a simple short-term plan.

I wrote:

Spiritual goals

I will attend church regularly whether I feel like it or not

I will read my Bible daily

I will pray daily

Social goals

I will do an act of kindness for someone at least once a week

Physical goals

I will exercise thirty minutes three times a week

Emotional goals

I will include in each day some relaxing enjoyable activity

I will display a "merry heart" even if it kills me!

Depending on the Lord for strength, I attended church regularly and continued as pianist. For weeks waves of nausea swept over me as I walked through the church door. There Cecil had cheerfully greeted folks and handed out bulletins. Many Sundays it took all the courage I could muster to open the car door and approach the church.

During the summer I was not working and I had time for reflection. About four months after Cecil's death I began thinking about ways to make it easier for my children at my death than it had been for me when Cecil died. It seemed that advance preparation would solve some of the difficult problems. I had frantically searched under the worst possible emotional circumstances for birth certificates, insurance papers, car titles, and the seeming multitude of required vital statistics. A will and a properly prepared letter to survivors could alleviate some of the frustration I had experienced.

First I met with an attorney and drew up my will. Next I took a manila folder and labeled it "Instructions to My Family at My Death." I included the following:

Name of my personal representative
Name and phone number of attorney to contact
Name and phone number of funeral home to contact
Details of service, if one is desired:
    Location of service
        Funeral home
        Church
    Type of service
        Open or closed casket
        Memorial service or funeral
    Theme of service
        Comfort and hope for survivors
        Celebration of homegoing
        Evangelistic
    Music requests
        Solos
        Congregational hymns

Readings
    Favorite passages of Scripture
    Poetry
Personnel desired
    Minister
    Soloists
    Organist
    Pallbearers
List of vital statistics needed for funeral home:
    Date of birth
    Father's name and birthplace
    Mother's maiden name and birthplace
    Length of residence in the state
    Social security number
    Location of, and deed to, cemetery plot
    Number of death certificates required
How to apply for Social Security death benefits
Location of health information (including vision and dental)
Location of personal papers:
    Will
    Birth certificate
    School and college diplomas
    Marriage certificate
Location of information for all assets:
    Life insurance policies
    Social security
    Pension
    Bank accounts (savings, checking, cancelled checks, bank books)
    Investments
Information about the house:
    Insurance
    Warranty deed

Location of information about the car:
    Registration
    Insurance
    Title
    Maintenance records
    Tire warranties
Income tax information:
    Location of previous and current year's records
    Tax preparer's name and phone number
    Credit card information

It is amazing how much changes in just one year, so I planned to update these instructions annually. Current, organized, and accessible information at the time of death would be a tremendous benefit to my survivors. It could help relieve some of the anxiety caused by the multitude of things requiring attention during a time of great emotional upheaval.

I felt a pleasing sense of accomplishment upon completion of my will and "instructions to family." It enhanced my confidence to know that I was able to organize my thoughts well enough to produce a useful, final product. Some of the mental confusion seemed to be lifting. I sensed a glimmer of hope and renewed determination to press forward in my quest to rebuild.

Six

I Will Never Leave You

I watched the late summer sun paint the western sky with breathtaking orange hues as it sank out of sight behind the horizon. It was peaceful sitting here on the porch in the warm evening breeze. Suddenly I realized that my summer vacation would end in a couple of weeks and I must return to work.

For the next few days my mind was totally preoccupied with obsessively exploring every possible (and impossible!) alternative to rejoining the working world. My kitchen table became strewn with papers displaying columns of figures estimating monthly expenses and calculations of income from full-time, four-day and three-day work weeks. What was the very least I could work and still make ends meet? I was determined to find out.

Resistance to returning to one's normal activities is a phase of the normal grieving process.

Something inside us resists returning to "business as usual." Our loss has been something special, and we feel that other people just do not understand how great the loss is. They talk about other things, and we are left alone with our sorrow. Everyone has forgotten our tragedy. Somebody has to keep the memory of it alive. We must not allow things to get back to normal again—it is much too painful. We are more comfortable in our grief than in the new unpredictable world.

There was a strange ambivalence associated with this resistance. On one hand I knew the return to work was best. It would give me a sense of belonging, structure, and emotional security. In spite of knowing this, my feet seemed firmly planted in opposition. What it finally boiled down to for me was a matter of economics. To eat I must work. It was that simple. So, resist as I might, there was no way out.

My peers genuinely tried to make smooth my transition back into the working world, and I was truly grateful. But as a new widow, raw from loss, I sensed how awkward my loss made others feel. I saw people as they approached me, trying to make up their minds whether "to say something about it or not." Those first few days I felt like becoming invisible rather than causing others this painful embarrassment. Tensions seemed to ease a little with each succeeding day, and gradually it became easier to face mornings—and people.

It was my seventh day of work and I was feeling proud of myself for making it this far. Paula and I were celebrating in the cafeteria with a cup of coffee. Instantly I was plunged into total panic by the message coming over the intercom.

"Mrs. Sissom, STAT!"

"Mrs. Sissom, STAT!"

Nausea swept over me. I trembled with fear.

"*Oh no, God. Not again! What now?*"

Something terrible must have happened to one of my children.

"*Help me, God, to face whatever it is.*"

I rushed to the nearest phone.

"Your house has been burglarized," said the carpenter

who had come to build my garage. He had found the back door open and badly damaged.

I phoned my boss and headed for home. With a vividness as if it were yesterday, I relived the trip down this same road to my tragedy five months before. As I drove along I began thinking about the stressful changes I had been facing.

"What is going to happen next, Lord? I feel like I am going under again, struggling with every ounce of strength. Help me!"

Just three weeks before, Paul had left for college in another state. The house seemed like a tomb. All those happy years of laughter and love with five people sharing our home had somehow faded into nothingness. The silence and loneliness was difficult to cope with. I could hardly stand the pain of walking past Paul's empty room, much less the agony of entering it.

Then another stressful event occurred when two weeks earlier the doctor had said, "That is cancer on your face. You must have it removed."

Thinking back to the evening before my cancer surgery, I recalled how the Lord had given me peace. The visiting pastor spoke on "How real is Christ to you?"

"Christ is as real as you want Him to be," he reminded us.

Then he asked, "How real do you want Him to be?"

He quoted Psalm 147:3–4: "He heals the brokenhearted, and binds up their wounds. He counts the number of the stars, He calls them all by name."

He read Psalm 103:14: "For He knows our frame; He remembers that we are dust."

He continued. "God knows when you are going to come to that hard place and He will see you through. He numbers your steps and permits trials to polish you up and make you shine. He knows what you will be doing at 10:00 a. m. tomorrow."

That statement startled me. *There is no possible way this visiting speaker could know that I have an appointment at 10:00 a. m. tomorrow to have the skin cancer removed.*

This message of comfort was divinely sent just at the right time—personally, to me—to counteract my apprehension and calm my fear.

"Thank You, God. You never fail. I can count on You to be there when I need You with just the right message for my individual need. What a kind, loving heavenly Father You are!"

"I need You again, Lord," I prayed as I turned into my driveway. *"Once more, please, give me strength for what is ahead."*

A mysteriously strange, foreboding feeling closed in on me as I entered my kitchen. It felt as if the presence of the burglar was still there. The door was split from top to bottom. A gouge was torn in the jamb from powerful prying. The kitchen floor was strewn with splintered glass.

I wonder what the rest of the house looks like?

My whole being resisted going into the other rooms, but I was soon pleasantly surprised to see everything intact—not one item seemed out of place.

Everything is here. But that doesn't make sense. The broken door. Something has to be missing.

Opening the closets I discovered that all the guns were gone.

The Belgian shotgun isn't here. Cecil would take Paul out in the back yard and let him pull the trigger when he was a little boy. Paul liked the loud blast it made. Cecil's rifle and the BB gun and rifle he had bought for Paul were gone. Nothing else had been taken. *"Thank You, Lord, it could have been so much worse."*

During the next few days, feelings of anger began to well up inside me.

Just think! Someone in my house, looking over the things that are precious to me, stealing my dead husband's treasures. How can one human being treat another so? What a display of cold heartlessness!

I felt like getting revenge on this culprit as I tried to imagine who it could be.

"Do not avenge yourselves . . .'Vengeance is Mine, I will repay,' says the Lord," came to mind.

"All right, Lord," I finally responded. *"You take care of it. I am forgetting that all I have really belongs to You, and forgetting what my Bible study on widows has taught me.*

"It's hard to trust You completely, Lord. Intellectually I know You are in control, that nothing can happen to me unless You allow it, and what You allow is best for me. But applying that to my life, resting on it, is so hard. I feel defenseless and afraid."

What if the burglar comes back?

Picking up my Bible I thumbed through the concordance.

Here's what I need . . . Psalm 4:8: "I will both lie down in peace, and sleep; for You alone, O Lord, make me dwell in safety," and Psalm 56:3: "Whenever I am afraid, I will trust in You."

I wrote those verses on an index card and put the card in my bedside stand. Reading my verses and praying for safety helped calm my fearful heart at bedtime and when I woke during those lonely nights. But my trust in God's protection was still weak and God used a series of incidents to strengthen my trust.

Fritz started barking frantically as I was preparing for bed late one evening. My heart began to race.

Someone is out there, that's his "people bark."

The phone rang.

"What are those lights in your woods?" my neighbor asked.

"Would you like my husband to run over before he goes to work?"

"Please," I responded anxiously.

He came to the door.

"Several men carrying lights and accompanied by hunting dogs thought your woods was ideal for coon hunting. They are gone now."

"Thank You, God, for protecting me and for kind, concerned neighbors."

The phone awakened me many times in the middle of the night.

"Hello, Hello"—

I could hear breathing, but no one would talk to me. Back to bed, another ring, the voiceless caller. Time to read my verses and pray.

God taught me another lesson through a series of problems I encountered with my mailbox. A car followed me up the driveway as I returned from work one sunny afternoon. I stepped out of the car near Fritz, hoping his presence would frighten this unknown visitor.

"Hello, I'm Tim. I came to tell you that I am the one who put the homemade bomb in your mailbox, the one that blew the whole side out of it. I have become a Christian since then and felt I should come to tell you I'm sorry. It was a dumb thing to do, someone could have been badly hurt. I will pay for a new box."

Mailbox vandalism was a great sport for teens in our country neighborhood. We had replaced our box five times in eight years. It had been smashed flat, riddled with bullet holes and filled with rotten eggs. I finally decided to carry the mailbox out to the road in the morning and back to the house

Instantly A Widow

every night. Then the attack on the post began. Cecil always built things in the strongest possible way, and the vandals discovered they could neither dislodge the post nor break it off. Instead they removed the part that held the box on the post. I found it in a ditch about a half mile from my home.

Why do teens continually destroy my property? They know I am a widow. This problem is wearing on me. It's a constant frustration.

"That mailbox belongs to God," my pastor reminded me. "Turn the problem over to Him. Let Him protect it."

I had prayed about it and was pleasantly surprised as I realized that God had prompted Tim to come and confess. We visited and rejoiced over his salvation. I commended him for coming to make amends. The attacks on my mailbox dwindled. Tim's visit helped inspire me to have more trust in God's protection. But just when I thought I was overcoming my fear several other experiences made me recognize my dependence on God for protection.

A nurse friend returned home from working second shift and surprised burglars in her house. She was stabbed and left for dead. This happened only a mile from my home, reviving the nagging fear within me.

Walking from the garage to the house when returning home alone at night sent shivers down my spine.

Is anyone hiding in the shadows?

What if I can't get the key in the door fast enough and someone attacks me?

"Keep me safe, Lord."

Upon returning home late one evening a van was backed into the end of my driveway . It was impossible to get around it. I flashed my bright lights on the driver. He flashed back. When I didn't move and he realized I really needed to get in, he slowly drove out.

"Thank You, Lord."

Several months later my fear was revived. "I thought you should know that someone tried to break into our house last evening while we were home," my new neighbor informed me.

The very next week, well after dark, a loud bang on the back door resounded through the house.

"Help me trust You, Lord, keep me safe."

It was not my usual pattern to listen to the radio at that time, but I was standing near it and decided to turn it on.

"Be not dismayed what-e'er be-tide, God will take care of you," was the first thing I heard. The comforting strains of that familiar hymn quieted me.

"You did it again, God. Just the right message at the right time to meet my individual need. Some day in heaven I hope to share this moment with that soloist." I never found out who or what banged on my door.

Soon after this series of fearful episodes, God gave me an opportunity to declare my faith in His protection. A non-Christian asked in genuine concern, "Aren't you afraid all by yourself?"

"At times," I admitted. "But God has allowed me to be in this situation, and I have to depend on Him to take care of me."

Very slowly my trust in God's protection was growing. Incident after incident demonstrated firsthand to me the protection God had promised. Some of those promises that became especially meaningful to me were: "Fear not, for I am with you. Be not dismayed, for I am your God . . . . For I, the Lord your God, will hold your right hand, saying to you, 'Fear not, I will help you' " (Isaiah 41:10, 13). I will never leave you nor forsake you" (Hebrews 13:5b). "Be anxious for nothing, but in everything by prayer and supplication, with thanksgiving, let your requests be made known to God. And the peace of God, which surpasses all understanding, will guard your hearts and minds through Christ Jesus" (Philippians 4:6–7). "Casting all your care upon Him, for He cares for you" (1 Peter 5:7). In fact I experienced a touch of excitement in watching God care for me.

It was time to prepare my annual Christmas letter. I was recalling the events of the past year. Suddenly I realized that I had been given trials during the past six months in the same areas that biblical Job had: *family*—my husband's death; *health*—skin cancer; *possessions*—my home was burglarized. The amount of my trouble seemed infinitesimal compared to Job's, but the *type* of trouble was similar.

Is it irreverent to suggest a feeling of identity with one who has inspired my faith during the depths of my despair? I hope not. Just think! God loved me enough to polish and shine me through these trials to make me more like the Lord Jesus.

I now enjoyed a closer, more precious relationship than I had known before.

I was determined not to cry in front of my children and spoil Christmas for them even though waves of sadness kept washing over me. I couldn't help recalling how the "little boy" in Cecil thoroughly enjoyed the excitement of the season. His curiosity would get the best of him, and we would catch him surveying the presents under the tree and shaking those marked for him. Pleasant memories lived on and nothing could snatch them from us—not even the lonely emptiness hanging over our first celebration without him. I put on a mask of happiness even though I felt sad and lonely inside. We went through the traditional Christmas activities of reading the Bible story of Jesus' birth, thanking God for the gift of his Son and then opening our presents. None of us talked about the sadness we felt. We wanted to protect each other from unhappiness during our Christmas celebration.

Rays of joy shone through the gloom from the knowledge that Cecil was in the presence of his Savior—the *real* reason for Christmas. We began to plan for a way to keep his memory and his dream alive.

SEVEN

Bringing Good Out of Tragedy

"Wouldn't it be nice if we could buy a new organ for our church?" Cecil asked about two years before his death.

I agreed that it would be nice, but there was no way we could afford it.

One Sunday each year my family returned to the church we had attended while we were growing up. My brother John delivered the morning message to the congregation that included visiting relatives and friends. After dinner we gathered around the organ and piano to sing hymns. Cecil always enjoyed the rich quality of music from the Rodgers organ. The fund for that organ had been established by a contribution in honor of my parents.

Twice, after coming home, Cecil remarked, "I wish we could buy a nice organ for *our* church."

Friends and relatives donated to a memorial fund at our church at the time of Cecil's death. Now a decision had to be made regarding the money. The children and I discussed Cecil's two main areas of interest in the church—children and music. Every Sunday he could be seen with a small child in his arms—how he loved them! He enjoyed singing in the choir and was especially proud of his family's ability to play musical instruments and sing. We remembered that it was a special musical number that touched Cecil's heart and convinced him to turn his life over to God eighteen years before.

We prayed for direction and discussed options. It seemed that a lasting, visible, and fitting memorial would be to resurrect Cecil's dream and place the memorial fund money into an organ fund. Cecil would be so pleased to have his dream turned into reality, and we felt an organ would be pleasing to God, as He would be given glory, worship, and praise through the realization of this dream.

The organ fund was established and a committee appointed. We visited the Rodgers Organ company for a demonstration, and we thrilled to the rich strains of harmony.

"If only the entire church family could see and hear this organ," we exclaimed.

"That can be arranged," the salesman replied.

We began making plans. Our excitement became contagious as we shared it through bulletin board displays, bulletin inserts, and announcements. The enthusiasm was shrouded with some doubt, however, because in our small congregation of twenty families were several unemployed men. It was recession time in the auto industry, the major employer of the men in our church. The purchase price of the organ was $16,500, and we only had $5,000 in the fund.

On a cold January Sunday we had the Rodgers organ in the church service for the people to see and hear. Carol was asked to play her offertory, first on the old organ and then on the Rodgers. The superior, rich tone of the Rodgers was clearly demonstrated.

Pledges began coming in. Could we really do it? Would

Cecil's dream come true? Would God provide the money in spite of the unemployed and retired members on fixed incomes? I felt an uplifting joy as I daringly dreamed of success.

Does Cecil know what is happening? Does God allow peeks at happy earthly occasions? I wondered.

In six weeks all pledges had been paid. Two weeks later the organ was installed. Cecil's dream was now reality. An engraved plate located to the left of the keyboard told the story. "IN LOVING MEMORY OF CECIL SISSOM, LOVED CHILDREN, LOVED MUSIC. DEDICATED THIS DAY TO THE GLORY OF GOD.

My brother, John, was guest organist for the dedication. He displayed complete mastery of the keyboard and the entire audience was captivated in his spell as he filled the church to the rafters with strains of classical greats and familiar sacred numbers. All sense of time escaped us as we entered into the mood of the music.

I was surprised and pleased to have present all my family and many of Cecil's relatives. While driving home after the dedication, my brother, Phillip, asked the question we all wondered about:

"Do you think God allowed Cecil to see these events today?"

We all hoped that He did. A quiet joy filled our hearts as we realized that as Cecil lived on in heaven, his dream lived on down here to glorify God.

After the organ project was completed, I experienced a letdown accompanied by bouts of loneliness. I knew I must not allow myself to sink into self-pity.

"The best antidote for loneliness is to reach out to others" was among the advice to widows that I had read. The Bible says it like this: "If you extend your soul to the hungry and satisfy the afflicted soul, then your light shall dawn in the darkness, and your darkness shall be as the noonday" (Isaiah 58:10).

I had attempted to carry out my goal to reach out to others with a kind deed weekly, and I needed some new ideas. I was standing in the garden looking at the beautiful results of my summer labor. Tomato vines were laden with scarlet juicy fruit. Delicious, plump, tender green beans were abundant. In the area orchards, luscious yellow peaches with brightly blushed cheeks were weighing the limbs nearly to the ground. Harvest time was always a joy, and I decided to preserve some of these tasty delights. So what if I were alone! I'd can in pints instead of quarts. Enthusiastically I washed the jars and lids. What satisfaction it gave me to fill each one with the colorful, delicious contents. I was having such a good time I hadn't realized how many jars I had filled—way too many for just me. I would share some with my children and then—what should I do with the rest?

I know what I'll do. The widow from church who is so despondent. I'll visit her and take her a box of filled jars.

It was great fun to select jars of bright yellow peaches, juicy red tomatoes, and plump green beans. A sense of abiding joy came from knowing I was truly helping another.

The secret of victory over self and sorrow is *outreach*, I thought. This was the beginning of many weekly visits that brought cheer to an elderly widow. And as I filled some of her lonely hours, my own loneliness was eased. I began to think of ways to bring cheer to others—mailing birthday and get-well cards, making phone calls to lonely shut-ins, inviting a widow for lunch. How grateful each person seemed for even the smallest act of kindness that said, "I care." Offering myself in an effort to assist the healing of others had a restorative effect on me. It was the most effective way I found to promote healing for my own lonely heart.

Instantly A Widow

My job gave me a sense of purpose, goals to achieve and challenges to meet. But a feeling of restlessness prevailed. It was hard to settle down and see a project to completion.

Many times during those busy days, I breathed a quick prayer, *"Give me wisdom, Lord, I need the right word, idea, or phrase for this writing assignment, and I can't think of it."* Time after time He answered my prayer.

Details of an exciting opportunity arrived in the mail one busy day, and I sincerely wanted to conquer the challenge. I had developed the hospital's Diabetic Patient Education Program and now there was an invitation to enter that program in competition for a national award. The application required long hours of thoughtful preparation. I found it very difficult to concentrate well enough to put a logical progression of thoughts on paper. It was a struggle, but enlisting my co-workers' help made it possible to mail the thick document before the deadline. I wanted desperately to win this recognition for our program, our hospital, and for my own personal satisfaction. I needed to prove to myself that I had not lost my professional competence.

A phone call conveyed the victorious news four months later. Our diabetic program had been one of eleven nationwide to receive a Leader Award for outstanding achievement in the provision of education for a specific target population. Our hospital of eighty-two beds was the smallest to win.

A beautiful bronze plaque was presented to me for the hospital during a conference at the Grand Traverse Hotel in Traverse City, Michigan, and I was awarded tuition for the first National Health Promotion Conference in Colorado Springs.

I had never been on an airplane, so the trip to Colorado was a real adventure. I viewed this as another test of how well I was doing in my recovery from bereavement. I didn't know a soul, but managed to find my way through busy airports, locate my seat on the plane, hold my shoulders erect, and display confidence outwardly. I absolutely loved the plane ride. It was exhilarating to fly in the sun above the clouds. What a thrill to look down on the tiny houses and cars and think how God can see all the people who are inside them and even know their thoughts. I was so thrilled with this fantastic adventure that I hated to leave the plane at Denver.

The conference included well-known speakers, displays, and opportunities to share with other educators from across the country. I even presented a display and discussion of our award-winning diabetic program. That gave my self-esteem a boost! I was determined to see some sights, so I paid the fare and took a Grayline tour of Pike's Peak. What an experience to ride those roads with no guardrails and look down the steep side of the beautiful mountain. I hired a cab and toured lovely Colorado Springs.

The flight home was just as exciting. We flew over cities aglow with beautiful lights penetrating the darkness. As we came in for a landing I reflected on the past week. It had been lonely—no one to share the excitement with—but I was beginning to feel a new sense of independence. *I must concentrate on the positive aspects of my situation.* I did not have to consult anyone when making decisions, and with no one waiting at home for supper to be prepared I could go shopping or to the library after work. I could even play the piano in the middle of the night if I wished! I felt a twinge of guilt over the happiness I felt as I contemplated my new freedom. Some sun was shining through the clouds of grief. I was eager for the next step on the uphill climb. I had no idea of the pain on the path ahead that was leading to an even closer relationship with God.

EIGHT

Your Maker Is Your Husband

"Four dollars, who'll give me five? I have five, who'll make it six?"

It was a sweltering August afternoon. The auctioneer was selling my husband's treasures. Both floors of the 30 x 50 foot barn Cecil built had been covered with equipment, tools, scrap lumber, and the results of Cecil's bent to collect junk. It took three years before I could bring myself to clear it out. In my attempt to be resourceful, I was looking for a way to earn income from the barn to help pay its own insurance and upkeep costs. I explored alternatives from boarding horses to starting a craft store, but ultimately decided on storing boats for the winter. One thing was certain: the present contents had to go.

Friends told me of an auctioneer and preparations were soon under way for the sale. I took advantage of this ideal time to sort through the attic, basement, and closets and include all items in the auction I could get along without. Men from the church came, placed a plank in the second floor door and we slid the upstairs contents down it onto the barnyard. Tractors, plows, cultivators, and harrows were displayed around the yard for inspection by potential buyers.

Just before the time the auction was to start, the auctioneer asked, "Aren't you excited?"

The absolute lack of emotion I displayed must have startled him.

"Not really," I said.

Doesn't he realize what pain it gives me to get rid of all my husband's possessions? These things are a part of who he was.

As the prized possessions left one by one I couldn't help wondering if Cecil knew what I was doing and if he was angry. Nevertheless it was a job that had to be done, and I was relieved to have this painful day behind me. The barn was one of the leftovers from Cecil's life that God used to help provide for me.

For many months after Cecil's death there was no song in my heart. Then all at once I felt the urge to sing *Under His Wings* on the way to work one morning. For many weeks I would turn my car in the direction of work and begin to sing:

Under His wings I am safely abiding,
Tho the night deepens and tempests are wild;
Still I can trust Him—I know He will keep me,
He has redeemed me and I am His child.
Under His wings, under His wings,
Who from His love can sever?
Under His wings my soul shall abide,
Safely abide forever.

Six weeks before Cecil's death, I had selected that song to sing in the church service with Kathy, a member of our church. Not in my wildest dreams could I have imagined as I sang it, that soon I would be finding refuge under His wings from the wild deep tempests of my sorrow.

During the same time before Cecil's death, I remarked to a friend how much I was enjoying my Bible reading in the Psalms. God's presence seemed close as I read the wonderful words of praise and comfort.

Singing my song on the way to work one morning, I began to recognize how God had prepared me for the coming crisis in my life through that hymn and my study in Psalms.

Three years later I again became aware of God's comforting nearness. It made me afraid.

Something terrible must be going to happen. God is drawing me close to Himself in preparation for another calamity. I wonder if something will go wrong with the eye surgery I'm facing.

The event God was preparing me for was not the eye surgery. That went well. Instead, a crisis started unfolding before my unbelieving eyes on Christmas Eve.

Janet phoned from Carol's condominium. "Something is wrong with Carol. She could barely make it up the steps. She is very short of breath and looks blue."

"Take her to the hospital emergency room right away," I responded.

The doctor thought she had pneumonia. He gave her an antibiotic and told her to contact her family doctor if she was not better by the day after Christmas. He said he heard a heart murmur and was concerned about her fast heartbeat. She did not improve. On December 26, Janet drove her to our family doctor. My activity was restricted during recovery from eye surgery so I stayed at home. Several tense hours passed while I waited for news. Janet returned home with the report that Carol had been admitted to the hospital and tests were being run.

Before long the doctor phoned. "Carol's problem is her heart. She is being transferred by ambulance to the care of a cardiologist at the medical center."

More waiting—no news. After several hours I could stand the suspense no longer. I phoned the cardiologist. A feeling of absolute terror surrounded me when he informed me, "Your daughter has a completely prolapsed mitral valve and must have open heart surgery at once."

Here I am miles away from my daughter, and she could be dying.

I shook with fear. Carol and I talked briefly by phone as they were preparing to take her to surgery.

"I'll come right away. I'll be praying for you while we wait for you to return from surgery."

I phoned my good friends, Netia and Chuck. They came immediately. We sat at the kitchen table and Chuck prayed before we left for the hospital. My entire body was trembling.

"*Oh, God,*" I prayed, "*Carol is the closest person on earth to me since Cecil's death. Is she going to be taken from me too?*" A feeling of terror paralyzed me again. "*Please, Lord, bring her through this and make her well.*"

The five hours in the waiting room seemed endless. I felt acute loneliness without the support of my husband. Loving friends came and sat with our family. I prayed and waited—waited and prayed. Finally the doctor appeared in the doorway. I quickly scanned his face for a clue to the message he was about to give me.

"Carol came through the surgery well," he said.

"*Thank You, God.*" *What a relief!*

"However," the doctor continued, "she will be very ill and her life will be hanging in the balance for forty-eight hours."

After another hour of waiting our family was allowed to see Carol. It was a terrible shock to see her so pale and unresponsive—tubes everywhere.

Panic gripped me. *Will she live? I must stay by her. I don't want to leave.*

Finally I was persuaded to return home. Sleep would not come. My heart was racing erratically, vibrating the bed with the hard pounding. Family and friends kept praying. I spent each day at the hospital. Friends offered to go for me.

"You need to rest so your eye will heal."

"No," I replied. "I have to be with Carol. I have to know she is all right."

By the second day after surgery, Carol started to show improvement and began to progress rapidly from that time on. God was answering our prayers.

Carol was discharged from the hospital in ten days—remarkable! She stayed with me for a month before returning to her condominium. It was a special time of sharing together. We thanked God for making doctors available at just the right time, doctors who had the special knowledge to treat her correctly. We thanked Him for sparing her life. Once again our family was confronted with the fragility of life and the necessity of being ready to meet God at any moment.

Four years had passed since Cecil's death, and ten months since Carol's surgery. It was a sunny October Sunday. I sat in church preparing my heart to worship God as the organ played softly. Suddenly I was aware of God's closeness. The very next week my mother collapsed and instantly went to her heavenly home. God had lovingly assured me in advance that He would be with me through this difficult time.

In November, I returned home from helping pack up all my mother's belongings, feeling abandoned and helpless. I thought how much I would miss Mother's daily prayers for me.

As I approached the house in the car, I noticed Fritz lying next to the side, coughing and wheezing. On closer examination I could see that his mouth was bleeding. I hurried into the house to phone the veterinarian. He suggested that I bring Fritz to his clinic right away.

After a short, unsuccessful course of antibiotics, the vet discovered that Fritz had inoperable cancer and there was no alternative but to put him to sleep. I stood in the clinic looking at Fritz and feeling slightly numb. Fritz was my husband's pet. They had been together constantly. Fritz seemed to realize an added responsibility to protect me after Cecil's death. He would sleep at the back door during the night and was more attentive and protective than he had been before. My last earthly protector was being taken away. There was no way out, so I signed the necessary papers and drove home without him.

Now I was absolutely, completely alone—*except for God.* I was in a situation of total dependence on Him to care for me. I had no choice. My faith in God would increase as I continued to learn first-hand how God protects the widow.

In retrospect I feel a deep gratefulness for the marvelous love and compassionate care of my Heavenly Father, who prepared me prior to the trials I would face in my loneliness. Each time He gave me confidence that He would be with me. Within nine years I had lost my father, father-in-law, husband, mother-in-law, my mother, experienced the near death of my daughter, my house had been burglarized, I was diagnosed with skin cancer, I had gone through eye surgery, and my son had married and left home. I turned to God for comfort and He became even more real to me.

Not only was I learning about God as the widow's protector, but He began to teach me valuable lessons about His role as my provider.

Early in my walk alone I became aware that all eyes were on me to see if the faith I proclaimed was real. Others were afraid for me when they asked how I was handling fear at night or how my finances were.

A husband was explaining how his wife had to get another educational degree so she would have financial security if he should be taken first in death. In response, my friend said in my hearing,

"Look at Ruth, God is taking care of her."

Yes, He is, I thought. *I have had everything I've needed—a home, food, clothes.*

But trusting in God as my provider had not come easily. In earlier years I always worried about money. I was actually basing my security on my meager bank account and in my ability to work and earn money. Then one day I discovered that the Bible says, "It is He who gives you power to get wealth" (Deuteronomy 8:18). This opened my eyes to the truth that God was giving me the strength to work, and He was providing me with a job to do. Without Him I was unable to provide for myself.

The next lesson God taught me about the folly of placing security in money came through a chilling financial crisis. I heard an advertisement on Christian radio that caught my attention. A financial adviser, Luis (not his real name) was talking about our responsibility as good stewards of the money God has entrusted to us.

"We are to make wise investments so our money will grow and we can contribute more to the Lord's work," he advised. "Come in for a free consultation," he invited.

I made an appointment. Luis said he was a Christian and he claimed that the Lord was really blessing him in his business. He handed me a fancy portfolio that boasted of his experience as a lecturer and a trusted financial adviser. He assured me that my money was safe with him because his firm handled tremendous amounts of money successfully.

"The Lord is taking care of me, I don't need your money," he responded when I asked about his fees.

His office was plush. His appearance was impeccable. He seemed exceptionally knowledgeable in finance and was a persuasive salesman. I was impressed and thought at last I had found a Christian financial adviser who really knew his business.

I explained my goal of retirement as soon as possible. I was looking for retirement income. Luis assured me he had the best plan available. He asked me about my assets and made a record of them. Then he explained the investments he recommended. They paid 23 percent, 17 percent and 14 percent interest. He emphasized the one paying 23 percent.

At my second appointment Luis presented me with a financial plan. "You must not leave your money in an annuity. I have seen annuities go under and people are left with a piece of paper that is worth nothing. In fact, this very thing happened to a couple who came to my office just last week. In addition to the insecurity of your annuity, the interest rate is twice as good with some of my investments."

Luis punched out unbelievable profits on his calculator. He convinced me and I signed papers to move money from my annuity to his investments. Luis emphasized how I would be able to contribute generously to God's work because of the exceptional interest I would be receiving. I went home feeling good about what I had done.

Just to be sure I was not making a mistake I phoned the better business bureau.

"We have no complaints in the three years he has been registered with us," they responded.

I felt confident that my decision was a good one.

Seven months later I took information for income tax preparation to Luis's office. It was then I learned that my investment was earning 7 percent and if I had left it in the annuity it would have earned 11 percent. Furthermore, because I had removed it from a tax sheltered annuity the total amount would be added to my income for that year. This resulted in additional tax. I had already lost a large portion of my investment in penalties and surrender charges. I also learned Luis had made a handsome profit from the money I moved to his investments.

"I am shocked to learn about the huge income tax payment. I don't know where I will get the money to pay it," I told him. "I don't understand why you advised me to move the money."

"This is good tax planning," he responded. "I'll loan you the money to pay your tax, don't worry about it. You have to have more confidence in me."

When these disastrous consequences came crashing down on me I felt powerless, abused, and resentful. It seemed incomprehensible that this trusted adviser could be so misleading, irresponsible, and uncaring. I had to lose a husband to receive the money that this deceitful trickster was using for his own gain. Later I learned that Luis had many unhappy clients and there was a class action suit pending against him.

Many sleepless nights full of agonizing prayer followed. There were consultations with attorneys, CPAs, and Luis with their resulting fees. Luis insisted he had done no wrong. The legal and financial hassles boggled my mind. Preoccupation with my financial woes made it difficult to deal with my demanding job. I felt like a stretched rubber band continually. Angry and distraught I turned to God for help.

"It's too much for me, Lord, You take over," I pleaded. *"The lessons You are teaching me through these experiences are painful to learn."*

I was learning the hard way that money is temporary and unstable, a thing of this world that can disappear without warning. My trust had to be in eternal things. Gradually I felt a calming of my anxiety as I surrendered to God the anger and vengeance I felt toward Luis. Ultimately Luis offered me a token payment. I decided to accept it and leave the rest to God. He would make things right in the end and take care of me as I put my trust in Him.

My message to all widows is *beware!* Only deal with financial advisers whose services have been used satisfactorily by your trusted friends. I have learned that the experience I had is quite common. Widows are typically unskilled in finance and are especially vulnerable to the swindlers.

The months of stress from financial upheaval coupled with my demanding job resulted in physical symptoms. I was seeing the doctor frequently.

"Your symptoms are stress related. You need to consider all your options. Can you manage financially without working?" he asked.

I took his advice and thought about my alternatives. First I considered returning to college for the marketing and business management training I needed to keep pace with my changing job. I enrolled for a business course, then I bought the textbook and read it. I decided that my natural abilities would not be used in the responsibilities of my evolving job. To find fulfillment I must change directions.

Next I put together a financial plan and consulted with a CPA and an attorney. They agreed that it was a sound one. I could manage financially without working full time. It would mean living frugally and perhaps working part time. I was willing to make those sacrifices in order to rebuild my health.

Instantly A Widow

"How do I know I'm doing the right thing, God," I asked. *"Am I acting irresponsibly to give up a good paying job that I believe You have provided for me?"*

The struggle continued for months. One day I would be confident that I was doing the right thing and the next day I wasn't sure. I prayed daily for wisdom. My health continued to deteriorate, and I finally informed my boss that I was leaving.

Immediately after I submitted my resignation, several large unexpected expenses threatened. This caused me to tremble, afraid that I couldn't make ends meet. Just at that time God gave me the message I needed through the study of Abraham in the Old Testament. God tested him in the area of provision, too. Because there was a famine in the land and Abraham doubted that God could supply his need, he went down to Egypt, where God had not told him to go. Finally he returned to the land of promise and to the will of God. He offered his nephew, Lot, first choice of the land before them. Lot chose the most fertile country, and Abraham got the leftovers. But he was in God's will now, and he knew that God would take care of him. He refused great wealth from the king of Sodom and then must have wondered if he had done the right thing, because God came to Abraham and said, "Do not be afraid, Abram. I am your shield, your exceedingly great reward." As I studied his struggles my faith increased. Abraham's God was my God too!

The message of a timely Sunday morning sermon came from Matthew 6: "Do not worry about your life, what you will eat or what you will drink; nor about your body, what you will put on . . . . Seek first the kingdom of God and His righteousness, and all these things shall be added to you" (vv. 25, 33). The truths taught in this message were just what I needed:

• God has promised that He will supply all my physical needs.

• As a Christian I am not to worry at all about how my basic needs will be met. These things are God's responsibility. This is stress I am not created to bear.

• The stress I am called to bear comes from my calling as a Christian—the challenge and excitement that comes from aggressively seeking to deepen my relationship with God.

The greatest truth I learned was that my security is in my relationship with God—not in money, possessions, or other people. He has said, "I shall not want" (Psalm 23). Contentment should be my mark as a Christian once I have put my financial affairs in the hands of my loving Heavenly Father. God delights to see me contented, well fed, safe, and flourishing under His care.

As soon as I asked God to help me place my security totally in Him, He amazed me with provision before my need was even known to me. Unexpected checks arrived before the unexpected expenses came. I found myself thanking God with the psalmist, "Blessed be the Lord who daily loads us with benefits." Calculating my monthly budget became a glorious experience as I realized how God had met each month's bills. Car repairs that could have been huge expenses surprisingly turned out to be minor problems in many instances. Health insurance benefits were suddenly available to me from another source just before they expired from my previous employer. A kind neighbor insisted on supplying me with free fresh eggs. Day by day I watched God work provisions out. I knew He promised to be the widow's provider but it never ceased to astonish me as I actually saw Him provide in countless ways for *me*.

Instantly A Widow

These experiences gave me a wonderful opportunity to share my faith with my acquaintances. I knew they were watching to see if I really believed God's Word. What was my attitude toward God's control of my life? Did I really believe that to die is gain, and that all things in my life are working together for good and conforming me to the image of God's Son? I felt a greater determination to allow God to display Himself through my life to others.

NINE

The Choice Is Mine

"You are to read all 909 chapters and keep a journal on them. There will be ten quizzes, a midterm, and a final exam."

Am I sure I want to go through with this?

In my determination to stay involved in intellectually stimulating activity I had registered for a college class in Old Testament Survey. My professional career had convinced me of the necessity of life-long learning. As a result I had taken classes, attended seminars, and read many career-related books, but this was the first class for college credit I had taken in thirty-four years.

I shuddered as the expectations were explained. Surveying my classmates I noticed that all but two or three appeared younger than I and all were, no doubt, more knowledgeable in the subject and used to studying and taking exams. My competitive spirit urged me to excel.

The first thing I did was count up the number of days until the journal was due and determine how many chapters had to be completed each day in order to finish on time. Repetition is the way I learn best, so each day began with reading the five chapters assigned for the weekly quiz. I constructed charts to organize the information and make it easier to memorize. With pounding heart and perspiring palms I received each test paper and did my best.

Fifteen weeks of daily persevering resulted in an "A" for the course. I surprised myself with that result! It was invigorating to learn so much information I could apply to my life for spiritual growth.

Reading became vitally important in my quest to stay interesting and conversant. It had always been one of my favorite pastimes and at last there was time to read all I wanted to. Simultaneously I had three or four books in various stages of completion scattered throughout the house, each one beckoning me to return to its exciting contents.

I longed to learn more about God and found several great books available in the church library. *Knowing God* by J. I. Packer, *The Normal Christian Life* by Watchman Nee, *The Pursuit of God* and *The Knowledge of the Holy* by A. W. Tozer were among those I enjoyed most.

For woman to woman reading I found inspiration from Catherine Marshall's *A Closer Walk* and *To Live Again*, Evelyn Christensen's *What Happens When Women Pray* and *Lord Change Me*, the inspiring poetry of Helen Steiner Rice, *Gift From The Sea* by Anne Morrow Lindberg and Elisabeth Elliot's books.

Nothing has helped like *A Shepherd Looks At Psalm 23* by Phillip Keller to give me a greater appreciation of God's care and concern for me as His "sheep."

Reading the Bible and dozens of great books has had a tremendous restorative impact on my life since becoming a widow.

Challenged by my reading, I felt a longing for some outlet of expression. My father had published poetry and my sister Marge seemed to have inherited all his talent. Still my gnawing desire to write something persisted. My hospital education job had included writing for the nursing newsletter

Instantly A Widow

and the hospital magazine. The Michigan Hospital Association had published my article on "Individualized Diabetic Education, Doing It Better" in *Michigan Hospitals Magazine*, their official publication. The national award for our diabetic education program had been won through a written presentation.

In a spurt of creative thought it came to me that I could write a book for my children. I would attempt to capture in print some of the precious times we shared as a family and remind my children of the great joy they had brought to my life. I could point out how each of them has wonderful uniqueness and great worth in God's sight. It would be their very own book written just for them, memories and thoughts preserved in print for them to reflect on and enjoy.

Before plunging into what seemed a monumental task, I visited the public library, read *Writer's Market,* and checked out several books on writing and publishing to learn more about what I was getting into. I decided to try.

It was great fun to recall our happy times together and reflect on how God had provided, protected, and helped us through the hard times. Some days I became so engrossed with my writing it was hard to stop for meals.

The inspiration for the title of my book came from a verse I had suddenly noticed in the Bible after Cecil's death. "I have no greater joy than to hear that my children walk in truth" (3 John 4). Truly my greatest joy next to my relationship with the Lord Jesus was to know that my children were living for God. I wrote that verse in the back of my Bible and thought about it often. *No Greater Joy* made a perfect title, reflecting the heartfelt message I wanted to convey to my children through my writing.

In five weeks my manuscript was completed. I couldn't wait to see the finished product. Beaming with excitement and anticipation I visited printers and bookbinders with my manuscript to obtain ideas and estimates. I wanted a classy hardbound volume my children would display proudly. The process of self-publishing my book was as challenging and stimulating as writing it. I learned about typesetting, print styles, types, colors and weights of paper, and binding styles.

With a pleasing sense of accomplishment I inspected the finished product. It had the smart professional look I wanted. One warm July day after a family picnic I presented each of my children their personalized copy of *No Greater Joy*. They seemed pleased and promised to treasure it.

Attending the college class, reading, and writing *No Greater Joy* were ways to carry out a goal I had set to participate in mentally stimulating activities and projects on a continuing basis. This was just one of the items in a "Plan For Living" I had formulated to keep me on the path to a meaningful life. The short list of goals I constructed early in my widowhood remains to this day as part of my expanded plan. Some of the additional items are:

Commit my life each morning to the purpose of glorifying Christ.

Spend time during daily Bible study to think about ways I can apply what I am reading to my life.

Stay involved in a daily routine that brings personal satisfaction.

Allow others to help me. My self-sufficiency is commendable, but not when it offends others or inhibits those who truly want to help.

Continually look for creative ways to use my skills, talents, education, personality, and other resources for the good of others.

I found that one way to enhance my spiritual goals was to keep a diary. I only write in it when there is something of significance such as a special need I have asked God to meet, a Bible verse or message that has been especially meaningful, circumstances that are evidences of God's care for me, or prayer requests and answers.

Another activity that helps me grow is to take a weekly spiritual inventory. This can be part of my diary. The busier I am the more I need this. I write down anything I think God may be teaching me and then plan how I can live better for Him the next week. Concentrating on only one area works best for me. For example: I notice myself saying negative things and criticizing others. My Bible study this week has taught me this is contrary to God's will. So for the coming week my goal is to refuse to say anything negative or criticize anyone. I will compliment at least one person every day and radiate positiveness. When I fail I confess to God and start over. At the end of the week I evaluate how well I've done and set goals for the coming week. My Bible study, prayer, diary, and spiritual inventory help keep my spiritual life on track.

Facing the stunning reality of death and the fragility of life changed my focus to living each day to the fullest with thanksgiving—an entirely new perspective. Things that were once major annoyances seem foolish and petty now. My priorities suddenly changed. Instead of keeping frantically busy, pouring my greatest energies into my job, I began to take stock of my life, to slow down and think about my life from the perspective of eternity. I began to recognize that what God puts in my path daily is His will for me. Dealing with interruptions and changes of plans is much easier when I accept them cheerfully as "God sent." It gives me great satisfaction to know that in this day, this hour, this place I am doing God's will.

The progress I was making in adjusting to living alone and in healing the deep wounds of grief did not prevent me from sinking into valleys of sadness. Joyous family occasions often made me melt in tears. We were a close family and the celebrations of birthdays, anniversaries, graduations, and other special events were highlights each year.

The marriage of our children and the arrival of grandchildren were events we had dreamed of sharing. No father was any prouder of his children than Cecil. I longed for him to be sitting beside me when our handsome son, Paul, now twenty-one years old, took lovely Jolene to be his bride. I could see Cecil beaming with pride as he escorted Janet, radiant in her beautiful bridal gown, down the aisle to marry Bob. My heart ached as the minister read a tribute to parents and Cecil was not there to share this moment with me.

When Rebecca was born to Paul and Jolene I couldn't help comparing Paul's amazement and expressions of pride to his father's similar reaction to the birth of our children. This special moment had arrived when he could have held his first grandchild—and he was *gone!*

Tears welled up in my eyes as I stood at the front of the church with Paul and Jolene as they dedicated Rebecca to God. Why couldn't Rebecca's grandpa have lived to enjoy this happy moment with us? Twenty months later Rebecca's brother Jonathan was born. I longed for Cecil to hold him. *Is he able to look down and enjoy what is happening?* I wondered.

Somehow in those children their grandpa lives on. I can imagine him looking down, grinning from ear to ear as he swells with pride. He is waiting for the day when he will be able to hug his grandchildren at last and hear the precious name he has never been called—Grandpa!

"How's life nine years after your husband's death?" my friends ask. "How are you coping? What activities are you involved in?"

"I'm very busy, not enough hours in the day to accomplish all I would like to. Life is full and exciting, and I'm enjoying each day. I play piano for Sunday school and organ for church, and I enjoy the many hours of practice. I crochet and knit sweaters for my family, and sell some of my handcraft projects. I have served on the church missions committee and coordinated mission projects for children. And I have helped build support groups for mothers of young children. There are so many good books to read, sometimes I have three or four going at the same time! I enjoy gardening: planting seeds, nurturing the plants, reaping the harvest, canning and freezing the delicious fruits and vegetables. Mowing my yard is a great time for reflection and meditation. My grandchildren are a wonderful joy. And I can't overlook the many relaxing hours I have spent exploring and touring on my outdoor bike and riding my indoor bike."

It is true that I have a grief that is not silenced, but it has become quieted with time. The loneliness hurts but I can dwell on it or fill my life with interesting activity—the choice is mine. The loss of affection and physical love is keenly felt. I wrestle with feelings of "what's the use?" and "who cares about my feminine attractiveness?" It is easy to withdraw in self-pity. Many days are a struggle between crushing defeatism and unwavering determination. I have the resources to be victorious. The choice is mine!

There is so much that has not been taken from me, much that is good and exciting. Best of all I have an inner strength that comes from the assurance that with God's help I have survived the worst thing that could happen to me, and I can rely on Him for the future.

It has taken a long time to reach this point, but life looks brighter than it has for a long time. Many widows have found a whole new world out there to explore, a world they didn't know existed prior to the death. I'm looking forward to a fulfilling future, too. I'm even daring enough to believe that the best is yet to come!

Experiencing the loss of a spouse hurts deeply. Recovery is very slow, and it is painful. I had to work through several phases of grief in order to make a full recovery. Each phase was healing. Little by little I became whole again and emerged a stronger person.

Faith plays a major role in the grief process, but not in the way I once believed. I first thought that a person with strong faith does not grieve. Now I see that faith was the stabilizing factor that helped me grieve more effectively, because I was helped by the conviction that God was with me during the dark days and that He would bring me out. "Yea, though I walk through the valley of the shadow of death, I will fear no evil; for You are with me."

When the very foundations of my life were crumbling under my feet the All Sufficient, Unchanging God was near to enclose me in His arms of love and see me through.

Annie Johnson Flint has put it so beautifully in the following poem. My sister Marge sent it to me while I was grieving. It was a great source of hope and comfort. I include it here in the hope that it will encourage other widows to have faith in God. He never fails.

At the Place of the Sea—Exodus 14:1

Have you come to the Red Sea place in your life,
Where, in spite of all you can do,
There is no way out, there is no way back,
There is no other way but through?
Then wait on the Lord, with a trust serene,
Till the night of your fear is gone;

He will send the winds, He will heap the floods,
When He says to your soul, "Go on!"
And His hand shall lead you through, clear through,
'Ere the watery walls roll down;
No wave can touch you, no foe can smite,
No mightiest sea can drown.
The tossing billows may rear their crests,
Their foam at your feet may break,
But over their bed you shall walk dry-shod
In the path that your Lord shall make.
In the morning watch, 'neath the lifted cloud,
You shall see but the Lord alone,
When He leads you forth from the place of the sea,
To a land that you have not known;
And your fears shall pass as your foes have passed,
You shall no more be afraid;
You shall sing His praise in a better place;
In a place that His hand hath made.

RESOURCES

Reading

Aldrich, Sandra P., *Living Through the Loss of Someone You Love* (Regal, 1990)

Baker, Don, *Heaven: A Glimpse of Your Future Home* (Multnomah, 1983)

Brite, Mary, *Triumph Over Tears, How to Help a Widow* (Nelson, 1979)

Canine, John, *The Challenge of Living* (Ball Publishers, 1983)

Chambers, Oswald, *My Utmost for His Highest* (Discovery House, 1989)

D'Arcy, Paula, *When Your Friend is Grieving* (Harold Shaw, 1990)

Decker, Bea, as told to Gladys Kooiman, *After the Flowers Have Gone* (Zondervan, 1973)

De Haan, M. R., *Broken Things: Why We Suffer* (Discovery House, 1977)

Elliot, Elisabeth, *Loneliness* (Bethany House, 1987)

Holmes, Marjorie, *To Help You Through the Hurting* (Doubleday, 1983)

Hunt, Gladys, *Close to Home: Reflections on Living and Dying* (Discovery House, 1990)

Jensen, Maxine Dowd, *Beginning Again: How the Widow Finds New Life Beyond Sorrow* (Baker, 1977)

Keller, Philip, *A Shepherd Looks at Psalm 23* (Zondervan, 1970)

Kuenning, Delores, *Helping People Through Grief* (Bethany, 1987)

Lewis, C. S., *A Grief Observed* (Bantam Books, 1961)

Marshall, Catherine, *A Closer Walk* (Guideposts, 1986)

Marshall, Catherine, *To Live Again* (Mc Graw-Hill, 1957)

Maughon, Martha, *Why Am I Crying? A Helpful and Honest Look at Depression* (Discovery House, 1983)

Mc Gee, J. Vernon, *How To Have Fellowship With God* (Thru The Bible Books)

Mc Gee, J. Vernon, *Why Do God's Children Suffer?* (Thru the Bible Books)

Nye, Miriam Baker, *But I Never Thought He'd Die* (Westminster, 1978)

Raley, Helen Thames, *To Those Who Wait For Morning: Thoughts About Being a Widow* (Word, 1980)

Rankin, Peg, *Yet Will I Trust Him* (Regal, 1980)

Sanders, J. Oswald, *Facing Loneliness* (Discovery House, 1988)

Westburg, Granger, *Good Grief* (Fortress, 1971)

Wiersbe, Warren, *Why Us? When Bad Things Happen to God's People* (Revell, 1984)

Yancey, Philip, *Disappointment With God* (Zondervan, 1988)

Yancey, Philip, *Where is God When it Hurts?* (Zondervan, 1977)

National Organizations

THEOS (They Help Each Other Spiritually)
1301 Clark Building.
717 Liberty Avenue
Pittsburgh, PA 15222
(412) 471-7779

Will provide list of chapters in your state upon request. Offers the newly widowed a magazine series called *Survivor's Outreach*.

Widowed Persons Service
c/o Leo Baldwin, Coordinator
National Retired Teachers Association
1909 K. Street, N.W.
Washington, D.C. 20049

Has groups in fifty-five U. S. cities. Uses specially-trained widows and widowers to reach out to the newly widowed.

NOTE TO THE READER

The publisher invites you to share your response to the message of this book by writing Discovery House Publishers, P.O. Box 3566, Grand Rapids, MI 49501, U.S.A. or by calling 1-800-283-8333. For information about other Discovery House publications, contact us at the same address and phone number.